START BEFORE YOU'RE READY

During the ten years I worked for Richard Branson I was fortunate to work with some of the best entrepreneurs in the world. The one characteristic that sums them up is tenacity. To say yes when others say no. To zig when others zag. Mick and his book are founded on this principle and I recommend it to anyone looking for a story to inspire and most importantly to succeed.

—**David Baxby**, Managing Director, Wesfarmers Industrials & Safety, Former CEO Virgin

When looking for success you need the drive and tenacity to overcome all the obstacles that come into your life and your business, and Mick has these in spades. Watch this space…

— **Janine Allis**, founder, Boost Juice

Life is short. In *Start Before You're Ready*, Mick tells us how to make the most of it.

— **Patrick Schmidt**, CEO The Iconic, Co-CEO Global Fashion Group

Start Before You're Ready is a book that is full of practical wisdom and a good dose of motivation to get you going on your next adventure, challenge or goal. Mick's story of turning from a boy with many challenges to a man with many successes is both enjoyable and engaging.

—**Stuart Cook**, former CEO, Zambrero Restaurants

Most entrepreneurial journeys are full of twists and turns—but when you keep a clear focus on why and where you intend to be then they become distant memories fast. How good of Mick to share his journey so we can learn from his twists and turns.

— **Naomi Simson**, founder, Red Balloon, co-founder, Big Red Group, Shark on *Shark Tank*

Mick takes us on his own journey and shares great insights on how he personally overcame challenges to create, innovate and make his business viable. The result is an authentic road map to gaining greater self-confidence and some great reminders on how to handle set backs!

— **Andrew Banks**, founder, Morgan & Banks and Talent2 International, Shark on *Shark Tank*

Mick has a never-give-up attitude and in my opinion, loves to solve problems that others may struggle with. He was born to be an entrepreneur and it was this creative attitude that helped us sell 4 seasons of DundasFit in David Jones. Working alongside Mick taught me that any problem or situation I get into in business can be solved one step at a time. Mick has a natural ability to stay calm and composed and not let big decisions cloud his judgment and he is always sharp no matter the time of day or the pressure of a decision. Mick won't stop, so listen to his advice and hold on!

— **Jason Dundas**, Australian TV host and entrepreneur

Mick wears his heart on his sleeve, and his passion and commitment shine through, in his new book on how he has overcome significant challenges, both personal and business related. In *Start Before Your'e Ready*, Mick summarises his lessons learned in an easy-to-read manner that will be certain to add value to any inspiring entrepreneur."

— **Clifford Rosenberg,** Managing Director S.E. Asia & Australia NZ, LinkedIn (2011-2017)

When Mick Spencer started out in business he started an entirely new business model for apparel. Why? He just didn't know the old model. Normally, clothing has a 6-12 month cycle. Design a lot of clothing you think your customer wants, go out and make it in advance using lots of your own money and then put it in multiple stores and try to sell it to them and hope someone buys it. Repeat. It's been done like that for about a hundred years. When Mick Spencer started he didn't know this model. He was too young! So he just started his own model that made a lot more sense. Let the customer, whether a big corporate client or a small sports club, use technology to upload and customise exactly what they want, use the same digital technology to print the fabrics and make it within weeks or even days, and deliver it overnight wherever they are—and the client has paid for it in advance. Brilliant! This book shows how the old business models can and should be challenged, especially if you have the drive to succeed like Mick Spencer.

— **Derek O'Neill,** CEO, Billabong (2003-2011)

There's no doubt any business, large or small, can benefit from Mick's 'start before you're ready' approach. I know ours has, and I'm looking forward to our continued partnership and entrepreneurial approach together.

— **Doug Swan,** CEO, Workwear Group (Wesfarmers)

What a great read! Mick's engaging story is full of actions, steps and tips for life and business success as we read about his experiences in pursuing his goals, getting out of his comfort zone and 'making the most of life.'

— **Glen Richards,** founder and CEO,
Greencross, Shark, *Shark Tank*

Micky Spencer is the definition of a dream-achiever. For anyone, diving into the deep end is a risk but this man is proof that when you persevere and work hard, you get there. I'm sure in his eyes he's only just getting started.

— **Adam Hyde & Rueban Styles,** Peking Duk—13x ARIA
Platinum Recording Artists

Mick's personal account of his journey to date demonstrates the passion, imagination and drive that can encourage young entrepreneurs to think about their future world in a different way.

—**Kate Driver**, Deputy Director and General Manager, Questacon, Australia's National science and technology centre

Each year, you meet people that stand out from others. Then you meet people who stand out from those that stand out. Mick is one of those people. His energy, enthusiasm and positivity is hard to contain. Having him put some of that energy, enthusiasm and positivity into his book makes for a fascinating—and thought provoking—read.

—**Fraser Henderson**, co-founder, Propel Funeral Partners, founder, Millbank Advisory, former partner, Minter Ellison

Start Before You're Ready is a well written motivational book full of stories and ideas for those who want to succeed in life.

—**Graham (Skroo) Turner**, founder and CEO, Flight Centre

START BEFORE YOU'RE READY

The Young Entrepreneur's Guide to Extraordinary Success in Work and Life

MICK SPENCER

WILEY

First published in 2019 by John Wiley & Sons Australia, Ltd
42 McDougall St, Milton Qld 4064

Office also in Melbourne

Typeset in 11/15 pt Sabon LT Std

A catalogue record for this book is available from the National Library of Australia

Cover Design: Wiley

Cover image: © Fidan Farajullayeva/Shutterstock

Author Photo: Simon Schulster

Internal graphics: © AntiMartina/Getty Images

Printed in Singapore by C.O.S. Printers Pte Ltd

10 9 8 7 6 5 4 3 2 1

Disclaimer

CONTENTS

FOREWORD BY HAP KLOPP

FOUNDER OF THE NORTH FACE

Throughout my life as an entrepreneur, adventurer, father, friend, leader, and philanthropist, I have repeatedly started my endeavours before I was ready. I have adventured into the unknown, taking The North Face from a dream of getting people further into the forests to what is globally known as the most popular adventure brand, grossing well over $2.5B USD per annum. I've adventured into the unknown, I've employed many thousands of staff and many went on to run major outdoor companies of their own. And I had the good fortune to share all these adventures with two amazing children, three grandchildren and a loving, supportive wife.

I had a real purpose in my career—to create a 'triple bottom line business.' One committed equally to the goals of profits, environment and society. Central to my vision was to preserve and protect the wilderness that surrounds us. I knew that if people went deep into the wilderness, they'd see the world in a really truly amazing way and understand the need for wilderness. As Eliot Porter once wrote, 'In Wilderness is the preservation of Earth.' I fervently believe that being a purpose-based business was the essential ingredient that allowed us to take The North Face from an idea for technical outdoor products to becoming a global fashion statement.

Through all my myriad of experiences, I learned there is no textbook for life. There is no one formula for success. You'll often find yourself in situations where you need to let intuition and gut feelings guide your direction. And, that's OK. Whether in the unknown mountain ranges of Patagonia, or the board room of New York, we as people grow when we're out of our comfort zone. And I believe that is where all the truly, valuable and disruptive ideas come from.

I met Mick a few years back. He reached out to me and I couldn't help but be drawn to his energy in creating something that I had always been passionate about—building something truly great. Because his vision encompassed using technology to disrupt the apparel industry which I knew so well it was especially intriguing. By the time we talked through his outline for offering customers a fantastic design delivery service, something that no big brand had yet been able to master, I was hooked.

I remember our first chat on Skype from his tiny attic office. I was energized by the OTG concept and its all-encompassing purpose, mission and execution. I did ask myself, how could a 21-year-old kid with no apparel background and only $150 figure out this concept? But his enthusiasm, his attention to detail and his lack of fear convinced be that he might just be one of those magical people who really could dent the universe, so I offered to contribute if he needed me. Over the years, I've mentored Mick, helped guide some grand, and difficult, decisions, and seen his journey. What a great pleasure it's been to see that growth in him as a person, and in OTG, which will be a major global brand that we'll all know and enjoy in the not too distant future.

When organisations get large, they slow. They stop innovating. They get too comfortable and they lose their nimbleness. They become risk averse and atrophy. They are afraid of failure but learn that the biggest failure of all is doing nothing. *Start Before You're Ready* is the ultimate ethos for life, and a reminder to kick ourselves in the backside and get going—because one can't wait until things are perfect; they rarely ever are. With the accelerating pace of society there is no longer time for perfect information. Mick's ethos, outlined in this book, provides the courage to take risks and gives a road map to help us as we throw ourselves into situations head first and learn on the go.

Despite incredible adversity, Mick has prospered. He's built a highly scaleable company, a stellar team, and an incredible consumer product. He didn't graduate with multiple degrees. He was not an expert in his field. Nor did he have the capital that most businesses do. Mick and his team have succeeded against all odds. They've started before they were ready, connecting vision and purpose. As you will read, Mick learned and learned well—by doing. The real way to live life.

With Mick's debut book, you will understand how to start right now, no matter what the odds. He shows how to get your mind and purpose aligned. How to paint the picture on where you want to be and how to get there. As Mick and I both believe: we can all be much more than we are today. Life is about adventuring beyond the unknown, and starting before you're truly ready.

Hap Klopp
Founder and 20-Year CEO, THE NORTH FACE
Author of *Almost—12 electric years chasing a Silicon Valley dream*
Hult University Lecturer on Entrepreneurship and Innovation

ACKNOWLEDGEMENTS

My partner Alicia—You are my waking inspiration every single day of our lives. You're my constant inspiration and I cannot wait for our future. The times we've shared are just the start of the journey ahead.

My father Greg, for telling me to never let fear stand in the way of anything and to give life my best shot.

My mother Cathy, for supporting every single step and motion of my life to date.

My brother Nathan, who has inspired me daily to give life my all, no matter what the circumstance. You've guided the light for me on too many occasions.

My sister Alicia, who has inspired me, showed me what is possible and reminds me why family is so important.

My mentors over the years—Chris, Hap, Chris & Bob, Derek, Paul, Baxby, Rainbow, Patrick and all those in between—you have been my real-life university and I wouldn't be here without your help in understanding the journey and what it all means.

My staff and suppliers, past and present; you know who you are. Thank you. For backing me, for every day guiding my vision of a different breed of business, and for putting up with my antics, obsession and curiosity.

Finally, I'd like to thank the naysayers, the teachers and the bullies for their constant reinforcement that I was not worthy of success because I was so different! You have been my underlying motivation to succeed.

INTRODUCTION

In November 2015 I was selected to pitch on *Shark Tank* Australia, a TV show millions of Australians watch. On the show, business owners pitch to five multimillionaires (the 'sharks'), hoping to impress them enough that they will invest their own money into the person's business.

Janine Allis (founder of the $400 million company Boost Juice) was mentoring me at the time, and recommended I apply. When they called to say they wanted me to audition I was thrilled, but unsure. How much time would this take? I was in the middle of a crushing workload closing our first investors into the company and travelling to China to see our suppliers, while still doing all my other tasks as CEO. But I knew I had to give it a shot.

I arrived at the audition feeling nervous. I wasn't used to the awkward, 'remember your pitch, word for word, in two minutes'–style presentations. I dug deep and made it happen, nailing my memorised pitch. Two weeks later they called to say they wanted me to come and pitch to the sharks on the show!

I worked long hours refining my pitch so it would have the desired impact. The morning of filming I had to arrive in Sydney at 4.30 to prepare the set. I was lucky to have Kris, one of my original teammates at ONTHEGO®, help me set up before the sharks arrived. Then I had to get makeup done and iron my clothes while reviewing my pitch again and again. It was nerve-racking.

'Mick Spencer—OTG—you have five minutes.'

My heart was beating at 150 beats per minute! 'Dig deep, Mick. Let's do this!' I thought to myself. The five minutes ticked by and then I was walking down the tunnel, greeted by the big timber doors and oriental carpet at the end. I walked through, and there were the five lurking sharks.

This is the pitch I gave to the sharks on 6 May 2016.

> Hi sharks. My name is Mick Spencer and I'm the founder and managing director of ONTHEGO sports.
>
> Four years ago a sports event came to me with a big problem. They had presold 400 cycling jerseys and needed them in under four weeks. The problem was that a staff member had left without ordering the jerseys, so they were stuck. No-one in the world could manufacture them in less than 10 weeks. I promised them I'd do it, and I found a way. And when I did, I uncovered an even bigger problem: thousands of retailers, teams and schools all had the same problem. There's a growing need for custom-made sportswear delivered fast, but it was always a challenging process.
>
> So with $150 to my name, in 2012 I backed myself and founded ONTHEGO to combine the things I was passionate about: building a global sports brand and giving back to those in need through our one4one initiative.
>
> Today we allow customers globally to design their own sportswear beyond what they ever thought was possible. Clients such as Ironman, David Jones, GoPro and over 3500 organisations use ONTHEGO. Just in the last year, we shipped over 25 000 products across 10 countries.

> We have the likes of Richard Branson, Ironman athletes, professional sports teams and clubs use ONTHEGO. We're also now extremely proud to have a line exclusively stocked in David Jones retailers in collaboration with TV celebrity Jason Dundas.
>
> Further to our online customisation and e-commerce, we've now developed the revolutionary OTG customised station: an innovative kiosk that will allow customers to go into a store, design their own product, while still maintaining a physical experience. A multichannel retailer that doesn't hold stock.
>
> We created unique technology and a vertical supply chain that encompasses everything from start to finish. So customers can have a seamless design experience—anywhere and from any device.
>
> With growth of over 80 per cent this year we expect to exceed sales of $1.5 million.
>
> With these growth rates and reorders, contracts and a big pipeline, we expect to be doing over $20 million in sales in 2020.
>
> To demonstrate how the brand works, just two weeks ago, when I discovered I'd be on your show, I jumped on our website and designed each and every one of you a custom product based on your product. So I'll let you come up and have a look…

There was silence, making my heart lurch. Then the sharks launched into questions, followed by negotiations. I walked out with a $600 000 investment! I'd done it! I'd negotiated the biggest deal of the season on *Shark Tank*! But would it be what I thought?

TAKE A MOMENT

Throughout the book you'll notice plenty of pages like this that ask you to stop, take a moment and write some things down.

But if you're not the type who writes in books, you can download the PDFs for all of these at:

onthegosports.com.au/book

PART I
MY STORY

IF YOU CAN
FALL IN LOVE WITH
THE THRILL OF NERVES
IF YOU CAN FALL IN
LOVE WITH BEING
OUTSIDE OF YOUR
COMFORT ZONE
YOU CAN DO
ANYTHING

CHAPTER 1

CONQUERING CHALLENGES FROM AN EARLY AGE

I was born with significant short-sightedness. I couldn't see anything for the first six months of my life, though it wasn't until several instances of bumping into walls, corners and terracotta pots that my parents realised something was definitely not right. I was diagnosed with short-sighted eyesight at –17, two points away from being completely blind.

I needed coke-bottle-thick glasses, and to bullies at school I was an easy target. When I was in Grade 3 my family moved from the suburbs to the inner city of Canberra, which meant I had to change schools. I was short and fat as a kid, nervously pushing my thick glasses up to keep them on my nose. I quickly became 'four eyes fatty'. I felt alone and scared, rejected by society and rejected by myself. I only had one friend, Tom, who knew me from my previous school. He was a cool kid and his acceptance of me helped. However, the kids in the years above still threw things at me as I walked home. And at lunchtime they always chose me to knock over on the oval; one would kneel down behind me and another would shove me so I would trip backwards and fall over his friend. I was the laughing-stock. I tried to act like it was funny and like it didn't get to me.

From early on I realised that school wasn't a place where I would succeed. My –17 eyesight meant I struggled to see the board, and I had problems concentrating and difficulty reading. Dyslexia and a big dose of ADHD provided a difficult learning curve.

What I did learn from school was to distrust details, and the system: the educational system, the lessons, the standardisation, even some of my teachers. I felt boxed in, asked to conform to something I knew I could never live up to. School was teaching me to see the world from inside a box—a box that everything had to fit in. But the real world isn't like that. Everybody is an individual. Everyone has interests and intellect and motivations, yet we're taught by a system that tries to jam us into its box.

Come high school I had to catch the public bus, and the public school kids spat on me and threw rubbish at me. Every day I would cop it, occasionally bursting into tears once I was home. I tried a lot of things, like keeping to myself and trying to blend in, but I didn't have much luck. My confidence was destroyed, and it tore up my parents. Dad always said: 'Be the bigger man; it's all part of the journey. Remember, Mick: every dog has its day'. However, it reached a point that made Dad change tack. 'It's time you turned around and insulted them back. Let them know they can't go on saying and doing these things.' I agreed. I was so fed up. The next time they picked on me I fired a highly insulting remark at the biggest bully on the bus, and he never had a go at me again. However, my confidence was still totally knocked.

Life outside of my comfort zone

By the age of 12 I wouldn't go out on weekends at all, not even to see friends at their houses. I was too frightened. It was safe inside the house, and there was no way I was going to venture out. Thankfully, my parents' mission was to have their kid change his attitude, and they wouldn't take no for an answer. On one particular Saturday they gave me $50 and said, 'We know it's scary for you, and we know what's going on, but you can't continue thinking the entire world is a scary place'. I was told to get on a bus, go to new places, and use the money I was given to explore and discover. I didn't even have a mobile! I was scared, of course, and didn't want to go. 'You're going,' Dad said, 'and I don't want to see you back here until after 5 pm tonight.'

I was petrified. I had never felt more out of my comfort zone. I gingerly got on the bus and began exploring different areas in Canberra. Even though I felt scared, there was something else—it was thrilling! I loved it! That day is responsible for my constant addiction to adventure, to finding new things and to operating outside of my comfort zone. That butterfly feeling you get…I love it. It's where life starts. That day taught me the importance of starting before you're ready. How often do we stay where we're comfortable, too fearful to venture out? We're lulled into comfort because it's nice. It's the café we're familiar with, the friends we've had for years, the job we're used to. But staying in our comfort zone cuts us off from finding new amazing cafés, from expanding our network with new awesome friends, from having a career we really love that reaches its potential. When we're comfortable in a routine, in doing what we know, we don't get to have the empowering experience of learning, and of surprising ourselves. Remember, humans have successfully built cities; we expanded from Africa to every inhabitable landmass; we invented the wheel and electricity; we harnessed oil to be fuel. We have smartphones in our pockets, medicines that save lives. And all of this was created by people who stepped out of what they knew into the unknown. At times it was dangerous, or scary. It was always uncertain. But that's where we grow! We felt the fear, and did it anyway. We started *before* we were ready. Sometimes it's our parents who will give us a kick to get going, and sometimes it's our partner, or our boss—but sometimes we need to give *ourselves* a great big kick and get moving. If you can fall in love with the thrill of nerves—if you can fall in love with being outside of your comfort zone—you can do anything.

That's the gift my parents gave me that day.

I changed from my coke-bottle-thick glasses to contacts, which meant I could finally play contact sports. I joined rugby and absolutely loved it! It quickly became my passion. Growth spurts and exercise meant I lost the fat, and the team camaraderie built a lot of confidence in me. Life was starting to be really great.

Then, one day when I was 13, I was on the rugby pitch and I felt my heart beat rapidly. It felt like a butterfly on steroids was flapping in my chest. It was weird. I felt short of breath and thought it best to leave the rugby pitch. A parent of one of the players was a doctor, and she counted my heartbeat, which should have been sitting at between 80 and 120 beats per minute. Mine was at 300 beats per minute. After 10 minutes, my heart flicked back into its normal rhythm, but my body was exhausted and I was in shock. Mum took me straight to the doctor, and he was perplexed that a 13-year-old, fit, healthy boy could have his heart beat at 300 beats per minute for 10 minutes. He told me to go straight to hospital for cardiac programming done to see what was going on. 'Shit, have I got something life-threatening?' I thought. I was scared.

Mum and Dad drove me the three-hour journey to Westmead Hospital in Sydney, where I was given a false heart attack to see what my heart would do, through which it was discovered I have a condition called supraventricular tachycardia (SVT). Ventricular tachycardia (VT) can kill you, so I was very lucky that I only had *supra*ventricular tachycardia. SVT essentially means that I have an extra pathway in my heart which misses the normal rhythm of the beat under stress. Imagine an electrical system with a fault so that rather than beating steadily, it shoots off into the extra pathway, sending it to beat at 250 to 300 beats per minute.

It's very rare for young people to get SVT, plus I was fit and healthy, which made it even more peculiar. They also discovered I have a weird heart in that it's very big, with a very low resting heart rate of 40 (most people have a resting heart rate of 60 to 100).

The specialists weren't 100 per cent sure it *was* SVT, so we were left in the unknown: could it be life threatening? It was scary for my family and for me. I had to see a cardiologist in Canberra every three months for them to monitor me, and I had to sleep and shower with a Holter monitor for three days to make sure my rhythms were monitored while I slept. It wasn't fun. It wasn't so much that I was afraid of dying, it was more the fact of being young and having to go to the eye doctor, and then having to see the cardiologist every three months. I just wanted to be a normal, healthy 13-year-old who didn't have to have regular check-ups. I hate hospitals, and to this day

I have a fear of sickness. And I wanted to know where I stood with my condition. I was living life out of my comfort zone every day to just get by. Nothing was easy. I had to quickly learn patience, perseverance and determination.

Whenever I tried to exercise, my heartbeat would become erratic and I was forced to stop playing rugby. I could no longer take part in my new-found passion. I wasn't passionate about anything they were teaching us at school—it was my love of sport that had kept me on the straight and narrow. Now that I had to stop rugby and be careful when exercising, what was I going to do?

From one passion to another

I turned my focus to earning money. I loved that having money allowed me to do some really cool things I had always wanted to do. The legal age to work in Australia was 14 years and 9 months, and my sister (who is five years older than me) worked at McDonald's as a shift manager and was able to get me a job working under her there. I loved every minute of it. My glasses continually fogged up from the kitchen's steam, but it was great working with people older than me and I loved the sense of belonging I felt. Working in a team gave me that sense of camaraderie that sport had. A sense I had been longing for. And I had money! Working there taught me so many lessons about management and business, and propelled me to appreciate work and how people come together to accomplish something.

With my growing confidence I became more talkative at school, cracking jokes in class to make everyone laugh and to stir things up. I think this came from wanting to be the centre of attention and because of the big insecurities I had about myself. I was known for asking my teachers silly questions, which most of them didn't appreciate. But I thought many of my questions were relevant, like when I would ask how certain maths and English problems could be applied to the real world. A few teachers saw through my act and appreciated my unorthodox thinking (and my jokes), but overall I felt school was only a place to have fun and build relationships. For me, it wasn't a place to study. I never got great marks. In fact, the only good marks I received were in PE, health and, funnily enough, business.

Soon after I began working at McDonald's with my sister, I started washing the windows of local shops and of the cars parked outside. I was on the pavement with the street kids and the homeless, asking people how their day was and if I could help them with their groceries—and, 'Oh, by the way, do you need your car windows washed?' I became quite successful at it. One time, a professional basketballer, Lauren Jackson (of Olympic, WNBL, WNBA and WBC fame), gave me $20 to wash the windows of her Mercedes, and when other people coming out of the shops saw this, they of course also wanted their car windows washed by... yours truly. Lauren became a weekly customer and the power of her influence taught me that if you're endorsed by someone who is well known and respected, you can capture a lot of sales.

As my window-washing reputation grew, I needed help. So I recruited three other kids to work for me. During the holidays we ramped it up, earning about $20 an hour. I loved buying the supplies and making sure 'my staff' were treated well and had something to drink.

I was also learning the value of a dollar, and I was drawn to garage sales. The commerce of used goods fascinated me. I'd get the newspaper on a Saturday and highlight all the garage sales I wanted to go to, and then I'd take some of the money I earned at work—say $50—and go buy up all the things I thought I could clean up and resell. I bought things like almost-new footy boots for $5 that I knew I could sell for $50, or a pack of CDs and DVDs for $10 that I knew I could sell separately for $10 each. I usually spent between $10 and $20 on an item and, after fixing it up, I'd resell it for anything up to $99. I was making good money for a teen. There were two channels for me to resell through: eBay was just coming online, and the classifieds section in the local newspaper. Every Tuesday you could post a free ad for items under $99, and on average I'd place anywhere from two to 10 classifieds, and then I'd wait for a call or email.

Mum and Dad thought I was crazy. Here were all these adults coming to the house on Tuesday evenings to give me money for second-hand goods. It humorously looked like I was running some sort of drug ring from the back shed. I would text and email potential buyers throughout the day, negotiating hard. I preferred written communication because I sounded very young on the phone. They were always surprised when a young kid answered the door saying, 'I'm Mick Spencer, your local classifieds expert'.

Once I was in the swing of it I made good money through eBay, even grossing $500 in one week at 13. It helped me buy an electric guitar in cash, which was a great moment. I'd planned for it, worked hard for it and eventually bought it. (I'd stopped receiving pocket money from my parents at 12 because I was making my own.) When I was 14, I found an MP3 player on eBay that I loved, and I knew it was best to put your bid on the items at the last minute. I would often set up three screens at once, set the highest amount I was willing to spend (a tip from Dad) and get ready for that last minute. This MP3 player was a beautiful, sleek, white-and-blue one that would fit in my pocket. I would be the cool kid. At the last minute I won it for $250! It was expensive, but I'd earned it. I contacted the seller, but there was no response. So I contacted them again, and again. Still no answer. Could this be real? I'd been hoaxed. (This was before eBay's strong seller security.) Someone had gotten an edge over me and taken my money. I was crushed, though it did teach me a valuable lesson: do your due diligence. It made me hungry, and prepared me emotionally for future failures. It didn't stop my love for the internet. My parents still call me the computer kid of the family. While I loved being outdoors and fit, I also loved connecting to people all around the world. Chatrooms, Bebo, MySpace—I loved anything internet based. I tried my hand at coding at a young age, building websites and profiles, and loved that too.

Another side hustle was at my school's swimming and athletic carnivals. I would bring a big esky of soft drinks and sell them, undercutting the canteen. It was completely illegal to do at school events, but the students loved the cheap drinks. There was an evident monopoly, and a disrupter was required! I happily stepped up to the plate.

In my teens, I always had two to three jobs at any point, and they were fantastic for developing the skills I would need later to build my own businesses. I worked at a grocery store, the post office, a local restaurant, on the floor of a chemist store, and later, delivering prescriptions to the elderly when I got my licence. My mum used to joke about how it always took me all day to do my prescription delivery rounds because I loved to stay and chat with the elderly people, who I knew didn't have many visitors.

Eventually I landed my dream job at a sports store. At each job I learned something new: how to interact with customers, how to place products, how the back office ran efficiently, and, most importantly, how to work with a team and collaborate.

At 14 I got into golf and by the time I was 18 I was playing off a handicap of five, which was nearing a potential career in the sport. I would be at the golf course from 5.30 to 8.30 every morning before school, then work from 4 to 6 after school, and then go back to the golf course after work to train. While training, I used to fish balls out of the lake and clean them to sell to golf clubs.

At the golf course some kids would pick on me. I'd be practising on the golf range and they would blatantly hit balls at me, and do stupid things like hide my golf clubs. It was petty—in fact it makes me laugh now—but at the time it knocked my confidence. Ultimately, I decided to give up the sport at 18 because I didn't think I was quite good enough to make a career out of it, and I was getting bored. I wanted new adventures and challenges.

In Grade 10, I completed my Personal Trainer Certificate at the gym, working there from 5.30 to 8.30 every morning as a personal trainer to do it. Everyone else going for a certificate was in their 20s or 30s. I was super passionate about health and wanted to know everything about it, so I wasted no time.

My moment of truth

Eventually the doctors confirmed that I definitely had SVT. It isn't life threatening, and would be more of a nuisance than anything else. That was a relief. However, they said that if I went into a 300 beats per minute rhythm and couldn't get out of it within 15 minutes I would have to rush to hospital so they could give me cardioversion (that's when they give your heart an electric shock).

One Thursday night when I was 17 I'd gone out with some mates, and the next day I went for a 5-kilometre run to shake off the hangover and to enjoy the beautiful day. My heart went into SVT. I walked straight home, counting my beats per minute: 240. I was totally exhausted. When your heart races at super speed, it circulates the blood around your body unnaturally fast. It takes everything out of you.

I did the exercises I'd been taught, but I couldn't get my heart out of the ultra rhythm. My Mum, Cathy, had worked as an emergency nurse for over 10 years, then as a clinical nurse and then a midwife. She's seen everything. When she says something, we all listen. 'You really need to be careful, Mick. We've got to go to hospital right now. This ultra rhythm can't last. We've got to get your heart cardioverted.'

Luckily, when you're in SVT you're rushed straight through emergency. They had to restart my heart by putting patches on my chest and giving my heart a brief electrical shock to bring it back to normal. It knocked me out. I woke up a few hours later and was discharged later that day.

My heart got stuck in ultra rhythm again when I was 19, and again I was rushed through and they shocked me into a normal rhythm. Both times it was scary. It made me less of a party animal, and much more conscious of my health.

Having my heart restarted actually boosted my confidence in general because it brought home the fact that life is too short to live in fear. I thought, 'Grow up, Mick. Make the most of life!' It just clicked. I started hustling more, forging my own life.

Moving on from school

After graduating from high school, I worked as a labourer for a year to save money for a gap year overseas. I worked at my dad's successful building company alongside my brother, Nathan, who is seven years older than me. While the work was tough and not much fun, I learned some great life lessons working with my brother. He taught me about organisation, money and focus. We had a lot of fun together.

Even though I could have continued in my dad's business and built a career there, I had a burning desire to live my own life. I wanted to prove myself and build my own future.

At this time all my school mates were saving to travel around Europe, but I wanted to do my own thing. I decided I wanted to intern at a sports camp in Hawaii: I love sports, I love the beach and I wanted time for myself to reflect on what I wanted to do. The sports camp said it didn't take interns, so I called the program coordinator.

'I know you don't take interns, but I'll tell you what. If you can accommodate me, I'll promise to work my arse off helping you to build the international program. I'll do the marketing and website for you. I know I can teach those kids something: team building, leadership and being the best you can be, no matter the odds. This is in my blood. Let me be your first international intern, please.'

They said yes! That further boosted my confidence—I'd made it happen. I was the master of my own destiny. That feeling was addictive. They would pay for half my flight, give me a shipping container as accommodation, a kitchen with bulk food and an old car for my days off. What more could a 20-year-old guy want?

I worked my arse off at the sports camp, and loved it. I was out of my comfort zone, having an adventure, and I got to have a real impact on some great kids. I loved how sports was bringing them all together. It was there that I realised the power of teams and the power of putting people in circumstances that bring them together towards a common goal. I was amazed at how the kids transformed; it was just awesome.

Hawaii was the place where ONTHEGO® Custom Apparel was truly born. It was there that I got a sense of what I wanted to do with my life. I wanted my work to involve sports, travel, adventure, technology and business. I wanted it to bring people together.

Every day matters

When I was 22, I suffered a new heart condition. I'd recently arrived home after travelling to China, and I hadn't gotten much sleep on the journey. I'd gone out for a cycle to stretch my legs when my heart started missing beats. I called Mum.

'It sounds like you're having heart palpitations, which are caused by exhaustion and dehydration. Drink fluids and rest, and see if it goes back into normal rhythm. If it doesn't, we'll go to the hospital.'

I went to bed extremely early, slept through the night, and woke up with my heart still missing beats. That's when I knew it was bad. I called Mum immediately.

'It's 7 am and it's still happening.'

'We're going to the hospital', she replied.

She drove me straight to emergency and I was rushed through. They diagnosed that it wasn't ectopic beats, it was atrial fibrillation (AF). All of the university interns came over to witness someone in their early 20s with AF because it was unheard of. Atrial fibrillation is a rapid, irregular heart rate that's very annoying and very tiring. At least with SVT it's a steady rise from normal to 90 bpm, to 120 bpm, to 140 bpm and then—*bang*—it goes to 250 bpm and you're in SVT. You're looking at your watch and counting, feeling it flutter in your chest. I've learned how to get myself out of SVT, at which point I'm instantly back to my normal rhythm. AF is different. It sticks around and your beats per minute are all over the place. They're irregular, sometimes fast, then slow, then fast. It can kill you. It's painful because you can't do anything except feel every beat and you become very conscious of every irregular heartbeat. And then you miss a beat. And then it goes *boom!* and you feel it up your throat. You're on the couch, unable to focus. You can't think. Blood isn't flowing around your body properly; it's not getting to your brain properly. You miss a beat. You beat in double time. It's the worst.

They gave me a drug to knock me out, and when I woke up I had severe chest pain from the electric shock they'd given me, which thankfully had got my heart back into its normal rhythm. 'You should have come to hospital last night', the doctor said. 'You're lucky to be alive: anything could have happened in your sleep.' He explained that your heart rate can kill you in your sleep. You can easily have a heart attack, or there's a risk of having a stroke with AF because it often creates blood clots.

I was 21 and being told I could have easily died the night before. It was a wake-up call. It made me reassess everything. Life is so short. It's scarily short, each moment insanely precious. Any second, we could be gone. At 17 and 19 I had had experts tell me that SVT wasn't going to kill me. I just had to be very careful it didn't last longer than 15 minutes. At the time, the experiences were full on because they had to restart my heart, but this was the closest I'd come to death.

The lesson to not take my health for granted hit me hard. I was in hospital among people who were older and sicker than me. Even though my heart wasn't great, I was still lucky. I realised just how *good* it is to breathe normally, to have a normal heart rate, to have all four limbs, to have energy. Being lucky to still be alive made me ask some important questions. What would I love to do with my future? I could die next week, or I could die in 100 years.

Every day matters, every moment counts

So what kind of life do I want to live? How do I want my future to look?

UNLESS YOU'RE
LIVING
DELIBERATELY
LIFE CAN FEEL LIKE
IT'S STUCK IN A RUT.
IT JUST KEEPS ON AS IT
HAS ALWAYS BEEN, WITH
NOTHING
CHANGING

CHAPTER 2

MAKING DREAMS COME TRUE

It was 2012 and I was choosing what to study at university. I thought a Sports Science degree would be a good marriage of my passions, but I had only gotten 44 per cent in my Grade 12 exams, and I needed at least 65 per cent to get into Sports Science. Surely I could find a way. I picked up the phone and called the convener, negotiating with him that I would help to better the look of the degree to other students, and would give as many volunteer hours as needed, in return for a place. He was impressed with my guts and that I was committed to adding value to them by helping out for free — so he gave me a place! I was pumped.

I set my sights on a 10-year goal of finishing my Sports Science degree, doing a Bachelor of Physiotherapy, and then opening a franchise network of physios around Australia. But just like I hadn't done well academically at school, university turned out to be no different. The one thing I did well was connect with people at my uni, both in my peer groups and among my teachers. My nickname from high school, 'Mick on the go', carried across to uni. I was known for my high energy and passion, and that I was always on the go. Socially, things were great. I was young, single and ambitious. I was learning a lot about life really quickly: learning what I wanted *and* what I didn't want.

I remember one special day, walking into a class and seeing blond hair, beautiful blue eyes and a gorgeous, smiling girl. I immediately introduced myself. Alicia was lively, fun, smart, beautiful and super chilled out. We became really close friends, studying together regularly and adventuring when we weren't at uni. She was my type of girl!

By the end of my first semester I felt unsatisfied. Sports Science just wasn't right for me. I decided to change to an International Business degree. I had the idea to brand coffee cups (an underutilised advertising space), or to create a printed T-shirt business. I thought 'On the Go' would be a great business name that could easily be applied to anything. I had $150 in my bank account, and I spent $142 of it registering the name. Around this time, I found out that Alicia had a boyfriend she had been with since her teens, which was disappointing because I really liked her. She had only seen us as friends, and when she realised that our relationship might be developing into more than that she thought it best to end our friendship. I thought she was amazing, but I accepted that nothing was going to happen with us. I had no hard feelings. In life that's what happens sometimes; you just have to say, 'It is what it is!'

Ten T-shirts and 400 jerseys

One day a uni friend came to me because he needed 10 printed T-shirts for his soccer club, and I'd been floating the idea of starting my On the Go printed T-shirts business. I told him I'd do it, and outsourced the printing while designing my 'ONTHEGO' logo. Once they were printed, Mum helped me rebadge all the labels with an 'ONTHEGO' label, and I packaged the T-shirts in beautiful boxes, then personally delivered them. My mate loved the T-shirts, and it turned out that one of the guys on his soccer team was involved in a cycling race the local council was organising and they needed jerseys. I received a call on a Thursday.

'Hi Mick. I've been forwarded your details by John. We have a cycling event coming up in just over three weeks, and we need 400-plus cycling jerseys manufactured by then. We thought they had been ordered, but our team member in procurement left his job without placing the order! We've researched everywhere globally, and only a few places say they can do it, but it will take them 12 to 14 weeks, and we only have three. We heard your company is quite experienced in this area of fast-turnaround custom products. We need a solution because we don't want to let the riders down — nor the charity involved!'

'That sounds like a big challenge, but I think I can help. I'll chat to production and the design team to see if this is something we can realistically do, and let you know tomorrow.'

I was in my parents' living room and Mum shook her head in exasperation. 'Mick, please be careful. Are you sure you can organise this? You can't even do up the button on your polo shirt, let alone manufacture an expensive fashion item!'

I just grinned. 'Leave it with me.'

Overnight I researched manufacturing, and after being told by numerous factories that I was crazy and had no chance of getting it done in three weeks, I finally found a factory in China who said they could do it if I gave them a hand with the digital files. Plus, the owner's brother-in-law was in Sydney! I couldn't believe my luck. I called the brother-in-law. His English was great, and he said they could do the order — but we were already behind schedule and the clock was ticking. He also explained that I would need to pay 50 per cent upfront, which was more than $5000—and I had only $500 to my name.

I thought it through. Considering these jerseys were custom made, I could ask for 50 per cent upfront from the council myself. Otherwise the risk would be too big. Dad had taught us kids to 'always know your risk'.

First thing on Friday morning I called the council back, my heart racing. 'We can do it in three weeks for you, but I'll need a 50 per cent deposit.'

'No worries. We'll transfer the full amount today. You'll have it this afternoon.'

I was stunned. I quickly got an invoice template from my brother, Nathan, and sent the invoice through. Then a lady from the council who worked in accounts called to say my ABN was wrong. 'I'll just put you through to accounts', I said. I paused, and putting on a different voice let her know that this was very strange and we would get the correct details through, but could she please not delay the deposit. In actual fact I didn't even know what an ABN was! I went to Google and quickly learned it stands for Australian Business Number. 'Yeah, right, Mick, you're really ready for this', I laughed. I called an accountant friend of mine who helped me register for my ABN straight away which, luckily, is a speedy process. That same day I was able to send through the corrected invoice and they transferred the money instantly. '*Wow!*' I thought. It was a real deal now. I had to make this happen.

I studied how to do the digital files for the factory, and worked like mad over the weekend to get them ready in time. On the Monday I had to transfer $5000 to the factory in China—to people I had never dealt with before. It was a *massive* leap of faith. You've got to roll the dice sometimes, and manage the risk the best you can. I knew the factory would not require the other 50 per cent until they had completed the order, so I went for it. My banking was not set up to do international transfers, so I had to go to the bank and set it up there, figure out the swift codes and transfer the $5000. Today our company pays tens of thousands of dollars a day to multiple countries overseas, with a dedicated accounts team, but back then everything was brand new to me.

I immediately sent the factory the digital files, that I had to learn myself, and worked with them on their workflow, studying every possible way we could do things differently to get the jerseys manufactured in the short time frame. Cycling jerseys are a complex garment to manufacture because of the technical material used, the number of panels, the function of the pattern required for a cyclist, the print process that diffuses the ink into fabric for the lifetime of the garment, and the technical features of having multiple panels with a lighter mesh that breathes — not to mention the three-quarter hidden zips. Complex, right?

Every day I learned more from the factory, and every day I was researching everything I needed to know. I spent hours and hours on the phone learning about freight, import licences and that I would have to pay customs duty. It was all new to me. It was exciting. It was a thrill to dive into the deep end, totally outside of everything familiar. I loved product, and I loved technology. I was working on my iPhone in between university lectures because I was midway through lectures and exams, and I was obsessively documenting every part of the supply chain to make sure every step was processed. I thought I could be onto something massive if I got this right.

I spent those three weeks living and breathing the project. In those three weeks I learned everything about the apparel industry: to pull it off I had to be an importer, a graphic designer, a fashion designer, a manufacturer, an import broker, a currency converter and a banker. By the end I had learned how the whole custom apparel manufacturing industry works, and I realised that anyone with the baggage of industry knowledge would never have taken on the project. My naivety for the industry and my passion and curiosity for the customer helped me to pioneer something very new for the market. It was an intense three weeks.

The cycling event was on a Saturday, and I had to pick up the jerseys from the DHL in Mascot, Sydney, at 6 am that day. I was praying my 1990 Ford Laser, which I had bought for $1500 the year before, would make the three-hour drive from Canberra to Mascot, and the two-hour drive from Mascot to Goulburn where the race was starting. I left at 3 am, got to Mascot on time, piled the car with the boxes of jerseys and took off for Goulburn. The charity cycling ride was massive: 1000 people riding together to raise money for a local leukemia foundation. An hour before start time everyone was still waiting for me. They were ready with their bikes and backpacks and supportive family and friends—but no cycling jerseys. My Ford Laser held out, and I arrived 30 minutes before start time to 400 people cheering madly. They couldn't believe I'd pulled it off, and were over the moon to have their jerseys. My mum couldn't believe it when I told her I'd made it just in the nick of time. She was always saying, 'What are you going to do if they don't turn up?!' I told her I knew they would.

It was moving to watch 400 people put on jerseys I had made happen. There was jubilation in the air, with cyclists wearing their branded 'Another OTG Product' jerseys with pride as they rode off to raise money for the charity. I saw my product as a part of bringing people together, a part of making money for charity, a part of being active and outdoors. I loved it. This business made sense to me.

The following week I was in an accounting class, bored out of my brains. My lecturer was explaining things too 'by the book', and I had the distinct feeling that he had never run a business before. I felt my business studies were flawed, only preparing me to become an employee of a big company, not self-dependent or entrepreneurial. I had had enough. I walked straight out of that accounting lecture and never went back. I had profited $25 000 from the cycling jersey order, which was enough capital to launch ONTHEGO as a proper business and tell my parents I was going to go fulltime to make this dream a reality. The economy was on its knees, but I had to go for it. If Goulburn Council had had this problem, surely there were others having the same problem? I had learned that the custom apparel industry was very 'top' heavy, with too many steps to be followed to get things done... and with the many steps getting in the way of the customer getting what they wanted, when they wanted.

There were the salespeople who would get the order, the designers, the pattern makers, the guys who made the digital files, the makers and mass producers, the shippers and too many questions back and forth between them—all of which blew out the time frame. What if everything could be seamless? What if customers could order fewer items more easily than ever before, and have their goods delivered quickly and *on time*, and in their own designs? I was sure technology could enable more efficiency in what seemed to be an old-school industry where the customer wasn't first. It was very hard for customers to get custom-designed products in a short time without ordering in the thousands of items to get exactly what they wanted. This was where I could make big things happen. The industry was ripe for disruption.

So I opened my first 'office'—a small, 4-square-metre space in Dad's old woodturning shed—nervous, but knowing I had to trust my instincts. To hotspot the internet, I had to hang my phone out the window because I couldn't access the house's Wi-Fi from inside the shed. But phone reception was never reliable: I would often have to run to the front of the house with my computer to get enough Wi-Fi to send and receive emails.

ONTHEGO® Custom Apparel (OTG) has been in business since 2012. The first three years were tough. I barely took an income. I was only just able to pay for rent and food. I never socialised unless people were paying for me. I put everything back into the business. And then we gained some real momentum! In 2016 (around the time I was on *Shark Tank*) we had seven staff and were doing $1 million in sales. Now we have over 40 team mates and ONTHEGO® is growing rapidly, with our enterprise valuation (EV) now in the tens of millions, and over 1 million products delivered across 710 cities.

Shark Tank: why I passed it up

After I did the deal on *Shark Tank* with three of the 'sharks', I was funnelled into the hands of one of the sharks' accounting/investment committees. They began a standard, thorough due-diligence check, which was highly intensive—and which took our small team a long time to complete.

I had agreed to sell them a discounted amount of equity on the basis that for 12 months they'd give a day a month of support to the business, but I was later told the sharks couldn't legally commit to time. This frustrated me as I'm a big fan of having people close to you when you need them. It's what early-stage companies need, and ironically what the sharks promised.

We finally completed due diligence in March 2016, and I was told the money would be transferred in June or July of that year. OTG was growing too quickly for us to continue waiting for their investment, and I was starting to feel that the sharks' values didn't align completely with mine, so I decided to thank them and move on.

As it turned out, not partnering with them was the right decision. They would have received 30 per cent of OTG—and our company's valuation today is around 16 times higher than it was at the time!

You only live once

'Start before you're ready' is one of my biggest mantras. I wasn't ready to manufacture 400 cycling jerseys in just over three weeks, but I dove into the deep end and made it happen.

Remember: the decision you make is always the right decision. Because when you decide to jump, you'll find a way to make it work. You'll surprise yourself. It's exciting, it's daunting, there's nerves and fear—but it's an adventure. Feeling that something is right in your gut, following your instinct and making things happen is part of the magic of life.

People often think that to launch a business you need huge capital and a business plan, or to work in a desired role you need X experience and Y credentials. The truth is, you don't. Some of the best businesses in the world started in a garage or dorm room, and people land jobs every day without having every set of criteria ticked. Apple started in a garage in 1976 when friends Steve Jobs and Steve Wozniak had the dream of making a personal computer. Dell Computers was started in 1984 in Texas by Michael Dell, who worked out of his university dorm room. Oprah Winfrey was born into a poor family in Mississippi, and at age 19 became a TV correspondent, despite a life of adversity. I got into uni despite having a score 16 per cent under the requisite. Never underestimate the power of school dropouts. Some of the most successful people I've worked with or employed didn't pass Year 12 or university. I look at some of the 'geniuses' I went to school with—who got a 99 per cent study score and were always under lights—still battling away. Then I compare them with great buddies of mine like Peking Duk (Australia's top DJs and multi-platinum record sellers), who were disruptive, like me, and ended up following their hearts—and by 28 years of age were killing it.

Starting before you're ready doesn't mean not bothering to prepare; it means instead of waiting, jump. Use the preparation you have and figure out the rest as you go. I took a leap when everyone was telling me to play it safe. I started long before I was ready, with no plan. But I had a vision, my habits and work ethic, my mind and my health—the things I could control.

The big, important changes in our lives are either due to our own making, or they happen through circumstances we could never foresee. Starting before you're ready is about the changes, decisions and commitments you make happen. Unless you're living deliberately, life can feel like it's stuck in a rut. It just keeps on as it has always been, with nothing changing. If you're feeling unhappy about it, it's time to change. It's easy to say, 'I'll save up some money and then I'll do that', or perhaps 'when I meet the right person, I'll make that change', or 'it's just not the right time right now'. The truth is that there is never a 'right' time, person or place. Sometimes things happen easily; sometimes they don't. The one constant is that the only person who can change your life is you. Accept your situation, make a commitment to take the leap and work for the life you want.

PART II
DESIGN YOUR LIFE FOR SUCCESS

PURPOSE COMES FROM WITHIN

IT'S A BURNING DESIRE IN YOUR HEART.

IT'S THAT FEELING YOU GET WHEN EVERYTHING YOU DO IS ALIGNED TO

A GREATER MEANING

CHAPTER 3

SHAPING YOUR FUTURE

This is going to sound like a cliché, but I mean it: your place in the world is unique. Even if you can't see it, you have to understand that you were born with a certain set of circumstances and genes, and a worldview that is yours and yours alone. You need to seize it. It's easier to live the norm and go along with the herd. But if I had done that, ONTHEGO (OTG) wouldn't exist. How could it? The world economy was on its knees; I didn't know what I was doing. But I seized my strengths, my unique abilities and viewpoint, and started before I was ready. I hustled. I saw my future and knew where I wanted to be. I grabbed life by the reins and I haven't let go since. 'But not everybody can do that', you may be thinking. Which is true. But you don't need to worry about everybody. You only need to worry about you. Can you do it? Can you see your future and do you know where you want to get to? Do you want to do it? Do you want to create a life where you live your purpose every day? Are you willing to sacrifice some TV time, some chill time, some drinking time, and apply yourself fully to this game of life? Are you willing to give it 120 per cent, so you can live a life that's full and fulfilling?

It's time to picture your future. It's easy to dream. We all love dreaming, but this is beyond idle dreams. It's about seeing real possible outcomes of who you are, what you care about, what you love doing and who you want to become.

When we struggle to get in touch with this, it's usually because we're out of touch with knowing who we really are. Some people go an entire lifetime not feeling they're truly living the life they want to lead. Give yourself the time and space to get in touch, to uncover your heart's curiosities, passions and the causes it cares about. Purpose comes from within: it's a burning desire in your heart. It's that feeling you get when everything you do is aligned to a greater meaning. If you put effort into your own dreaming, take yourself seriously, trust yourself and set markers, then you're going to find who you are and the future that you'd most like to reach.

What gets you out of bed every morning? Life is so short. Stop messing around. Yes, you're going to have days that are hard. But inevitably, if you love what you're doing, you're going to become a much better version of yourself.

I found, in both my personal and business life, that once I accepted what I wanted and began to go for it with all of my might, the universe began to open doors. It's not as mystical as it is practical: we often truly are our own worst enemies. Once we commit to our futures, we begin to see opportunities that we couldn't see before. We seek out when before we remained silent. We push ourselves to our limits and, hopefully, beyond.

TAKE A MOMENT

It's up to you to take hold of your future before someone else does. Write down now what you want.

- Do you want to start your own business?
- Do you want to land a job at X company in the next five years?
- Do you want to become a manager, or make a career change to something entirely new?
- Do you want to earn money from your art?
- Do you want to do a PhD?
- Where do you want to be a year from today? Five years from today? How about in 10 years' time?

JOT DOWN YOUR THOUGHTS HERE

– *start side flower business*

– *complete my PhD by June 2019*

With my severe near-sightedness I can barely see anything at night, even with glasses or contacts on. I'm as blind as a bat. (My fiancée instinctively grabs my hand when it gets dark, to lead me.) When I was a kid and my family was on holiday, camping, I remember needing to go to the toilet at night. Because I couldn't see a thing I had to envision the path in my mind. I'd walk step by step, seeing the twisting trail solely in my mind's eye. Sometimes I stumbled and kicked my shins, but I always got to my destination. Like that kid on the path, hurrying along, the adult me is hurrying along his own, self-created path. I envisioned the path I wanted to tread. What path do you want to tread?

What legacy will you leave?

When my business came to fruition and I started making a bigger impact in people's lives, I was taught the value of visualising your own funeral. What will your life look like at the end? What did you do? What did people think of you? What impact did you make? What do you really want to do in the world for others? Due to the rejection and bullying I experienced growing up I knew I wanted to be important in people's lives.

One of the biggest common traits I've seen in the successful individuals I have learned from is their strong sense of the legacy they want to leave when they pass away. Your legacy doesn't need to be a company, or stardom, or wealth.

TAKE A MOMENT

The key areas that successful individuals often reflect on and make note of regularly are:

- What legacy do you want to leave in your community, with your family, with your (current or potential future) partner and with your kids?
- What kind of person do you want to be known as when you pass away?
- What do you want people to think of when your name is mentioned?
- What kind of impact have you had on people's lives—career or personal?

Take a minute to write your answers to the above questions, giving yourself time to really think about them: if you were able to attend your own funeral, what would you want the main message of your life to be?

JOT DOWN YOUR THOUGHTS HERE

- *known for energy, never giving up*
- *pushed the limits*

Find your purpose

The definition of purpose is 'The reason for which something is done or created or for which something exists'.

People often ask, 'How do I find my purpose in my life?' I find it helpful to rephrase the question as, 'How do we accept ourselves?' When you accept yourself for who you are and what you have, everything starts to fall into place. Most people don't accept themselves, which causes inner pain and turmoil, and hinders them from connecting with what they care about most. We spend a lot of time focusing on what we don't have, rather than what we do. We try to fix our 'faults', rather than *accept who we are* and grow ourselves from there. It's hard to change a habit when behind it you are at war with yourself, trying to use willpower to 'force' yourself to 'be a better person'.

In school we're taught that we *mustn't* fail—in fact, failing is the worst outcome there is. If we fail a test, it effectively implies that *we*, ourselves, are a failure. This is completely untrue, but unfortunately the school system's understanding of failure raises people who hate themselves more and accept themselves less. Not only that, but the social pressure of school forces us to be something we're not. If we're not 'cool', we're not good enough, so we have to change to be accepted, driving the wedge even deeper. That's why, as soon as you come across this understanding of how we're brought up, it's essential to re-train your thinking so you can accept who you are today. Once you do, you'll find growing yourself from there much easier and more enjoyable. And with that, you'll awaken to your purpose. Finding purpose is a journey. And they say that to uncover the reason we're here, we need to love ourselves fully first.

So how can you accept yourself?

Early on I learned that there was nothing I could do about my poor eyesight. And there was nothing I could do about my heart condition. I was forced by circumstances to accept both—that was all I could do. Accept it, and learn to live with it. With this acceptance I quickly turned my focus to finding out what I *could* do, rather than dwelling on what I couldn't. Accepting the circumstances, accepting myself and choosing to take action on what was in my power to do, has fuelled my journey ever since.

MICK'S TIPS FOR FINDING YOUR PURPOSE

The fact is that we can all do *so* much more than we believe. Accept who you are and where you are, and re-train your brain to be on your side rather than judging you, and you'll realise just how far you can go.

Connect deeply with possibilities for your future, for your life, work and lifestyle, and you'll find yourself clear on your purpose.

Realise that it's time to love and nurture the great things about you. The things you haven't perfected are always a work in progress. That's the way of the world. Those who succeed are the ones who accept themselves for who they are—and who don't give a shit about the rest!

Purpose isn't something you can teach; it's not something you can come up with because you've been told it's a good idea to have. It needs to come from inside, from the heart. I found my purpose when I went through a lot of trauma and realised the power of bringing people together through sport and activity. It's what made me love my internship in Hawaii so much, and it's what makes me love the business I'm in so much.

At OTG, our purpose is to bring people together through custom apparel because we believe custom apparel provides a sense of community and a common set of beliefs and values. We further our purpose through our social impact projects where we give to communities in need through our grants. Charities and social groups apply for either money or apparel needs, and we choose who aligns best with our quarterly focus points and give them the funding and/or apparel. It's one of the most blissful things, seeing your company and your people do great work for other great people.

TAKE A MOMENT

Open a new note on your phone, or use the space provided below, and give yourself a moment to really reflect, and to write your answers to these questions:

- What really makes you tick?
- Given who you are, and where you are, and your work ethic and your interests, what would you like to make happen in your life?
- What purpose has perhaps subconsciously guided your decisions until now?

JOT DOWN YOUR THOUGHTS HERE

The goal in life is to find the collision of what you love, what you're great at, what the world needs and what you can be paid for. That's the sweet spot.

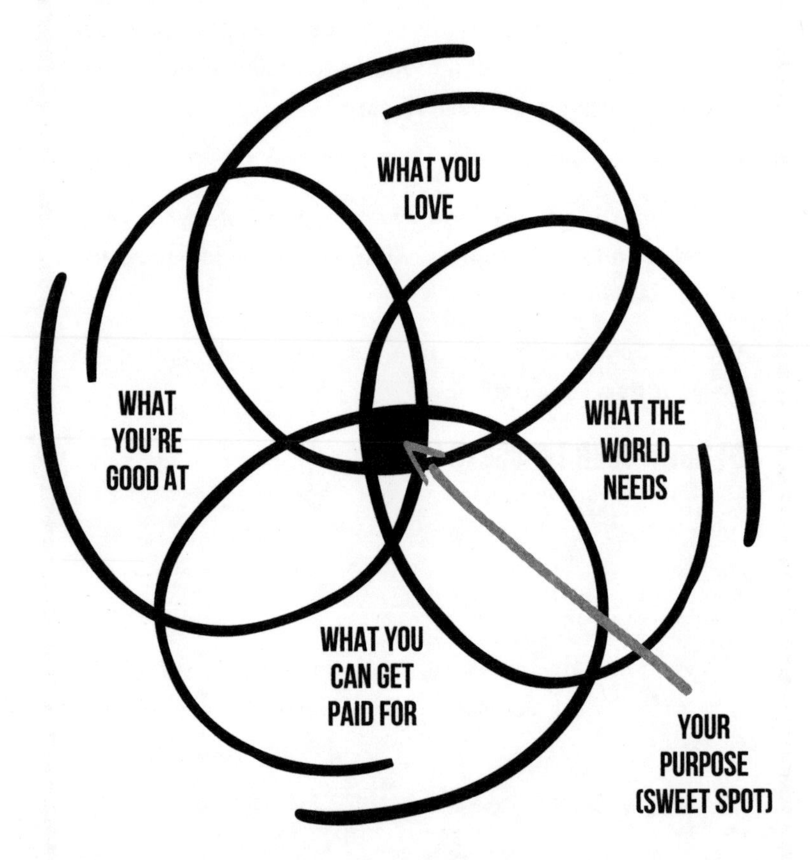

Love what you do

Building a business is tough. Building a great career is tough. Becoming a well-known artist is tough. There are moments of glory, but usually they are few and far between. In the early days of OTG I often wondered if all the hard work was worth it... and I always came back to something Steve Jobs once said. Every morning he'd ask himself, 'If today were the last day of my life, would I want to do what I am about to do today?' Whenever his answer was 'no' for several days in a row, he knew he had to change something.

For me the answer has remained a resounding 'yes'. If today were the last day of my life, I would want to be doing exactly what I'm doing now. I believe in it wholeheartedly.

If you can operate at the intersection of what you love doing and what you can do, and you're making an impact, then you have a great life ahead. And remember that it's a constantly evolving journey. It will likely change over the years, over the decades. All the best people I know in career and business are never settled—they love the journey of evolving what they love.

Believe in yourself

Know that you can accomplish things you previously thought were out of reach. You are smart enough. Resourceful enough. Committed. When I began OTG I knew nothing about the clothing and manufacturing process, but if I had been paralysed into thinking I couldn't do it, I would never have taken that first big order.

With acceptance for yourself flows a strong belief in your own abilities. Not a belief that things will work out the first time (they hardly ever do). Rather, a belief that when they don't work out, you'll figure out why, learn from it and try again. Believing in yourself is putting your faith in your ability to persist. To pick up the phone, and make the call. To apply for that job you really want even though you're not sure you have all the experience or skills they're looking for. To believe in yourself that you will get yourself in the zone, and nail the interview. And that if they call you back on Tuesday to say you didn't get the job, you believe in yourself still and set your sights on the next application and interview. Maybe you study that extra skill online, or get a short internship to build up experience. Believing in yourself is the foundation you have within yourself that no matter what, you have what it takes to make it happen.

When we don't have that strong belief in ourselves, it's often because we're too comfortable. You need to push yourself so you have the opportunity to surprise yourself with what you manage to do. Diving in the deep end builds your belief in yourself. Playing it safe keeps you wondering if you're actually capable. Put yourself into situations you aren't used to; do things you haven't done before. Nothing builds confidence more quickly than completing tasks and projects that are foreign or difficult. And that new-found confidence will transfer into other areas of your life. Remember that you once had to learn the things you find easy today, and things that are hard today will be easy in the future.

In an interview for a PBS documentary called *One Last Thing*, Steve Jobs said something that I found life-changing. He said that we're brought up to believe that the world is what it is and that we should simply fit into it. He called this 'a very limited life'. He said we should challenge this notion because 'everything around you that you call life, was made up by people that were no smarter than you' and that we should embrace life, change it, improve it and make our mark in this world. He concluded by saying, 'Once you learn that, you'll never be the same again'.

Trust that the dots will connect

Life is an interesting mix of planning and unpredictability. John Lennon once said, 'Life is what happens to you while you're busy making other plans'. Your plan might happen, or it might partly happen, or it could be totally sideswiped by another opportunity or by an event outside of your control. I've been sideswiped by my heart condition, by being let down in a big way by someone I hired, by fraud. But through it all I've kept my purpose and my vision constantly aligned and dialled. I've had enough things fall into place for me unexpectedly, too, to know and trust that all I need to do is keep going, and the dots will connect. The harder you work and the more passion you execute on, the closer you'll come to the right opportunities.

When I did my first capital raise, a few of the investors were really, really keen to invest in OTG. Raising capital is a fulltime job in itself, and I was working hard at it while still being CEO of OTG, which was at the time in intense start-up mode. It was *so* tough. I did a heap of preparation, nailed my pitch to the investors, answered all of their questions, and still they kept asking more and more questions. For weeks and weeks they were dragging me along, but I persisted. They were really keen to invest, and I was determined to close my first round of financing for the company.

On a 6 am flight to Sydney to spend the day meeting with the potential investors to get them, finally (and hopefully), to say 'yes, let's go ahead', I was pumped and exhausted. The woman in the seat next to me was a lovely lady called Juli who I chatted with before getting my laptop out to work. She saw the designs of apparel on my screen and was interested to know more about what I was doing. I enthusiastically shared everything: what we were doing, how exciting the growth was, how awesome the technology we were developing was. She was very impressed and asked for my card. 'Let's keep in touch.'

The meetings that day turned out to be a complete disappointment, with the investors still dragging on. I was near ready to give up. Raising capital, I'd discovered, is the hardest thing there is to do. It can be completely demoralising. You spend so much energy getting someone really pumped up, answering their 1000-plus expert questions, and then they turn around and say something like, 'We think you're a really great guy, but OTG just doesn't fit our current investment criteria'. Or, 'Thanks so much, Mick. We really love your enthusiasm, but we're just not sure that OTG will be successful like you think it will. Best of luck'. Or, 'Hi Mick, thanks a lot for meeting us today. We really enjoyed meeting you and learning about your company. We'll get back to you when we decide if we want to invest', to then wait weeks and weeks and hear nothing. I was feeling down.

A week later, I received an email from the lady I had met on my flight to Sydney. It read:

'Hey Mick, it's Juli. It was lovely to meet you on the aeroplane last week. If you're ever in need of capital, let me know. I've done some successful investments over time, and I'm a career doctor. I would be happy to invest in your business if you'd allow me.'

She didn't even know I was looking for capital! I couldn't believe it. I caught up with her for coffee, and she wrote us our first investment cheque the very next week. She has since grown her equity stake in OTG, and with the growth we've had she has made 10 times her investment, with her original stake now worth well over $1 million.

You never know what conversation, what meeting, which person, is going to help you dramatically. You never know who you will meet who will impact your journey. You never know if someone you helped out might make a difference later on. Trust that the dots will connect. Trust it'll all piece together. Yes, you're going to have a curvy journey getting there. But somehow, it will all fall into place.

ROUNDUP

- If you accept yourself for who you are and what you have, everything will start to fall into place.
- Believing in yourself means knowing that you have what it takes to make anything happen. It starts with loving yourself.
- Finding your purpose will help you uncover the reason you're here in this world—and remember, your purpose comes from the heart.
- Build your confidence in your abilities by completing tasks and projects that are out of your comfort zone.
- Remember that the 'sweet spot' is the intersection of what you love, what you're great at, what the world needs and what you can be paid for.
- The more passion you execute on, the closer you'll come to the right opportunities. But don't be fooled: it's hard work!

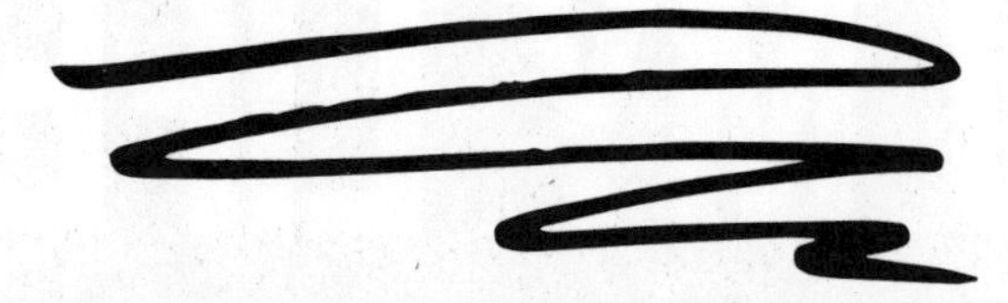

HOW MANY TIMES DO YOU GENUINELY LEAVE CONVERSATIONS WITH PEOPLE AND THINK

WOW

I'M NEVER GOING TO GET THAT TIME BACK

THAT ADDED NO VALUE TO MY LIFE?

CHAPTER 4

THE 4 Ps PHILOSOPHY

I am constantly designing my life for success, and my goal with this book is for you to do the same. I live each day deliberately, always checking in with myself to make sure I'm on track in all areas of my life. And my favourite way to do this is with the 4 Ps:

Purpose – People – Planet – Profit

I learned this philosophy a few years ago and instantly loved it. In fact, the 4 Ps (also known as the quadruple bottom line) have become my life philosophy, and though they're normally used in the context of business I use them in my personal life as well. A lot of people who I truly admire also use the 4 Ps.

You need all 4 Ps to live a balanced, successful life, and to have a good balance you need to be conscious of all four regularly. I'm constantly thinking, 'Am I living a good balance of the 4 Ps? Is this business decision aligned with the 4 Ps?' When I first told my fiancée about the 4 Ps and how I live them, she typed them up and framed them for me for my birthday and they're hanging on the wall in our bedroom.

Purpose

Purpose is so important. Before making decisions, pause and think: is this aligned to my purpose? Is this still coming from the heart, or am I getting too focused on earning money? Will this decision benefit more than just me?

At OTG we make all our business decisions, literally, at board level, from our *why*. Our *why* is ingrained in our values and stands on our wall. We hire and we fire off it, we align ourselves to it and we reflect on it regularly as a company.

People

The people around you will hugely affect you. Who do you want to be? Who is in your life? It's crucial to be around the right people, which means being really conscious of who you spend time with. Studies have shown that you'll earn the average of the five people closest to you, which is one way of measuring how we become like those we spend the most time with.

Ask yourself, 'Who am I around? Am I still learning, growing and powering ahead with the people who are around me?'

You need to be constantly reflecting on the people in your personal life and the people you work with, and aware of whether you're growing beyond their mindset by asking yourself, 'Am I finding that too many times when I'm with these people I'm not feeling a sense of empowerment, or that there's too much bitching and drama going on? Do they accept me and my journey? Are their judgements and little side comments starting to weigh me down?'

TAKE A MOMENT

Reflect on your *why*:

- If today was your last day on the planet, would you be happy with what you're doing? This will really open you up.
- Why are you truly doing what you're doing? Is it contributing to something bigger than yourself, and what is that?
- Do you really feel like you're genuine in what you do?

JOT DOWN YOUR THOUGHTS HERE

It's wise to know when it's time to transition to seeing some people less, and others more. Strengthen your relationships with amazing people because they affect every area of your life, from your emotions to your finances. People can seriously *grow* you, or *diminish* you. How many times do you genuinely leave conversations with people and think, 'Wow—I'm never going to get that time back. That added no value to my life'? Sometimes this is one of the hardest things to do: saying 'no' to people and politely moving on. I've had to do it multiple times.

One of my proudest and perhaps greatest achievements (in the sense that it propelled me to where I am today) was seeking out and building a solid support network of mentors, associates, executives, employees and friends. I found the best people I could in fields or careers I wanted to learn from, and I would ask to meet them for coffee. Picking their brains over coffee has taught me so much. My network consists of experts in mergers and acquisitions, intellectual property, research and development, tax incentives, financial modelling, angel investing, seed investing, software engineering, the technology of fabrics, branding, partnerships, customer relations, supply chains and many more. There are roughly 100 highly intelligent professionals, all successful in their own right, who I go to for advice, mentorship and guidance. These people are invaluable to me.

TAKE A MOMENT

On your phone, find the last 10 people you had contact with. Are they building value in your life?

The next time you go out with your 'gang', ask yourself whether these people are actually adding value to the parts of your life you want to be strong in. Are they making you feel like the best version of yourself?

Think deeply about who you want to be in one year's, three years' and five years' time. Are the people you're surrounding yourself with helping you get there?

What kind of people do you want to surround yourself with and learn from?

JOT DOWN YOUR THOUGHTS HERE

- *visionary, supportive of goals*
- *let me be me*

Planet

The planet is a beautiful place, but in our busy, urban lives we often lose touch with nature. I'm very interactive with nature. On a weekly basis, no matter where I am, I find time to be among it. Just three minutes from my home is bushland with amazing mountain bike trails. I ride there often! When my connection to nature is strong, I have a clear mind — it opens me up to be freer mentally, and to think differently. If I'm overly stressed, I go and chill in nature. I'll disconnect from social media and my emails by leaving my phone at home, and enjoy the muddy trails on my mountain bike, or surf in the sun or go fishing in the mountains with my dad and brother. Or on a Sunday morning my fiancée and I will leave our phones at home and have a barbeque in a nearby park. It's great. We must connect to nature.

To reach your goals in work and life you need to always be in the process of restoring yourself. And one of the best ways I've found is to have a strong connection to nature. It restores my wellbeing and helps me reconsider what's truly important. For example, I was recently on the Gold Coast to talk at a conference hosted at the casino. I'm not a casino kind of guy, so rather than sleeping in and getting up in time to do my speech, I got up an hour early and went to the beach. I enjoyed a run along the shore, and then dived in for a swim. The salt water and sun restored me and I felt rejuvenated and in the zone.

People don't know what nature can do for them until they experience it. When I take friends on a mountain bike ride they're always amazed at how good it feels to be outdoors, among the trees, doing exercise, breathing in the fresh air — with our phones left at home.

TAKE A MOMENT

- When was the last time you were in nature and looked at the sky and went, 'Ahh, this is beautiful'?
- What's your happy place? Do you have one?
- How many times a week could you go walking or running or riding in nature without your phone?
- Could you start going on a walk in nature each weekend? Jump on Google to find your closest nature reserve, and go for a walk there, leaving your phone in the car.

JOT DOWN YOUR THOUGHTS HERE

While in my personal life Planet is about making sure I'm spending enough regular time in nature to keep me grounded and refreshed, in my business it means making sure that what we do is sustainable. At OTG our division of merchandise is focused on building better environments, from inks to fabric and stitching to cutting, and we concentrate on sustainable practices that ensure the environment can flourish. Our internal ethical sourcing policy is called 'From Mill to Move — doing business the OTG way', meaning that from the fabric mill to our customers moving in our products, everything must be as sustainable as it can be. As we grow, we're also very conscious that we have an obligation to our environment, and are working on new ways to recycle material and used items that our customers return to us, such as last season's uniforms. We believe in a 'less is more' approach — while we love re-orders, we want our customers to be proud of their products and not have to always buy more. Customisation is great in that it gives the consumer confidence to build a product unique to them that no-one else has. We make 'fit for purpose' products, but using the best engineering we can. We also strictly audit our factories to ensure our ethical and environmental standards are met. We try to ensure our clothes live in cupboards for years in the future!

I also utilise nature to do exercise with potential new partners and employees. When I was in Vancouver (signing the Canadian hockey team for OTG to make their apparel), I learned that I'm not the only one who uses this as a way to get to know people. I had wanted to meet the founder of Lululemon forever, and had already reached out four times. While over there, I emailed his PA again and managed to get through! She said that the only time he was available was on his 5 am to 8 am hike of the Grand Mountain, and would I like to join him? I said 'Yes!' The night before, it snowed in so we couldn't do the hike, but I did get to meet him briefly anyway. He said that he used to take every new staff member for a hike up the mountain because getting them out of their comfort zone was the best way to get to know them well. I couldn't agree with him more.

Profit

This is all about wealth creation. Profit and cash is vital. You need money to support yourself, and if you have children, to support them. But it goes beyond you and your family — purpose needs profit to have a bigger impact. OTG has multiple charity initiatives, and our cash flow is the reason we can do that. It's exceptionally hard to help the world with no funds. If you've identified purpose within you, you've got great people around you and you're connected to mother nature, making a lot of money and accumulating wealth will enable you to do more. Which feels good, right?

The perfect balance

Finding the balance between the 4 Ps is like walking a tightrope: you're never going to keep a perfect balance. The important thing is to continually self-correct. And you may find that you need to go through a stage where for a period of a few months you live one P more than the others, which is fine as long as you're conscious of why you're doing it. Over the past six months, I've focused my time on profit, sacrificing my time in nature and social time. I've been fine with doing this because I knew that the amount I had to earn to get OTG to a certain point would take all my focus. It worked because throughout the six months I was still consciously reflecting on the 4 Ps, and I was constantly clear on why I was out of balance, focusing on profit. It's important to note that I did *not* sacrifice our value of using sustainably sourced materials or diminish our responsible manufacturing processes—I only sacrificed my own health, and some of my time socialising and in nature. You need to know what's okay to sacrifice, and what isn't.

There are many times in our lives—boy, I've had a few—where you're not balancing the 4 Ps right. You may be in a spot where you're too profit driven, and others fall down. Or vice versa, where you're spending time on purposeful activities but your profit activities fall down. It's important to reflect on how you're balancing these. Here are the questions I constantly ask myself to re-assess.

Which of the 4 Ps have you been spending most of your time, focus and money on? Are you naturally in tune with the importance of purpose, but needing to spend more time learning how to earn or raise more money so you can make a bigger impact with your purpose? Are you spending all of your free time socialising without spending any quality time in nature? Are you too focused on earning money, and feeling hollow because you haven't taken the time to connect with your purpose? I often see people who are way too busy to be a family person, or to be there to care for their loved ones. It's very unbalanced. They have all the money in the world, and I feel deeply sorry for them—they need to focus more on purpose, people and planet.

TAKE A MOMENT

Think about your perspective on profit:

- How can you be wealthy enough to live life on your own terms?
- How do you build wealth?
- What can that wealth do for you and for others?

JOT DOWN YOUR THOUGHTS HERE

– *how much wealth do you need?*

TAKE A MOMENT

Let's see if you're balancing the 4 Ps effectively.

- Are you feeling in tune with your purpose?
- Have you checked in with your family recently?
- Have you switched off your phone and gone into nature?
- Have you reviewed your financial goals?
- Who did you last call? Are you happy with them being in your life?

JOT DOWN YOUR THOUGHTS HERE

ROUNDUP

- Live each day deliberately by balancing your life around the 4 Ps: Purpose, People, Planet, Profit.
- Your purpose is your *why*: make sure it's ingrained in your values.
- Be conscious of who you spend time with by making sure the people you spend the most time with are helping you to learn, grow and power ahead.
- Having a strong connection to nature will restore your wellbeing and help you know what's truly important.
- You need money to survive, but accumulating wealth and knowledge is also about giving back to others, and to society.
- Make sure you know what's okay to sacrifice, and what isn't, to create a perfect balance.

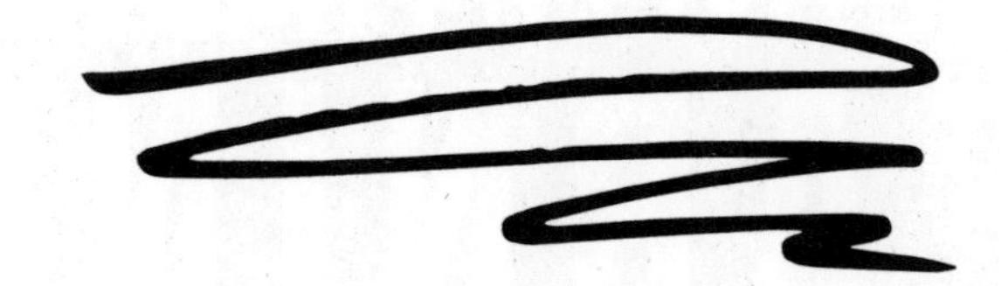

WHETHER YOU LEARN TO FURTHER YOUR EDUCATION, DO SOMETHING ATHLETIC OR LEARN A NEW LANGUAGE FOR FUN

IT DOESN'T MATTER

THE IMPORTANT THING IS TO ACTIVELY PRACTISE

LEARNING NEW THINGS

→

CHAPTER 5

MAKING EVERY MOMENT COUNT

'Make every moment count' is my definition of maximising every possible moment. Getting the most out of life, and your activities, means using your time wisely. It doesn't just happen. It requires planning and being very disciplined (most of the time, at least). Once you start, you turn it into a routine and then you have a chance to actually make this ethos subconscious. I'd like to share with you something that's very important to me: my most important habit and how I manage my time. People have often questioned how I get so much done: how I can do what I do. It's all about how you manage your day, time and activities—from the moment you open your eyes to when you close them to go to sleep.

Actively learn

Part of designing your life for success is building the habit of actively learning every week, or, even better, every day. Many people stop actively learning after school or university. Sure, we learn as we move through the adult world, and our jobs or business teach us as we go, but we often miss out on actively learning a new skill. Our brains are built to learn—we love to learn! It's what keeps us engaged in our careers and in life. If there was no challenge—if there was nothing new to learn day in day out—we'd be bored.

Learning is not only challenging, engaging and fun, it's empowering and humbling. If your confidence has been knocked, maybe by being bullied or retrenched, or due to staying in your comfort zone for too long, learning a new skill can empower and energise you. There's nothing as exciting as not being able to do something, then dedicating hours to learning it, and surprising yourself with your newfound ability! Learning is humbling because it takes you back to square one. Whenever I've had a big week of presentations, important meetings and closing deals, and I'm sitting in a class as a total beginner in Mandarin, I'm humbled.

I'm currently learning Mandarin because a lot of our factory partners are Chinese, and before Mandarin I was always learning something else on the side while running OTG. Over the past few years, I've learned to play the didgeridoo and the ukulele, and I've trained for and completed an Ironman and a marathon along the way. I've learned to code new technology languages and to invest in property and the stock market. I've studied neuro-linguistic programming (NLP) to understand the mind better, which has helped me tremendously in business and as a CEO. And, through OTG, I've learned how to run a successful business, hire staff, be a CEO and leader, raise capital, close big deals, pitch, present, constantly manage my time better, communicate clearly, use other people's money to grow their and my wealth, and more.

MICK'S TIPS FOR ACTIVELY LEARNING

- Make sure you know where you want to be and what (if anything) is holding you back from becoming who you want to be. Think about how you could get there.
- There's so much out there that you could be learning: online courses; reading peer to peer; listening to podcasts... find something that interests you and learn it. Whether you learn to further your education, to do something athletic or to learn a new language for fun, it doesn't matter. The important thing is to actively practise learning new things.
- Be genuinely interested in learning.

Make your habits support your future

My daily habits are essential for me to do the work I love, and there's great thought and effort behind every habit. Being the CEO of OTG is an intense role: it's very busy, and no two days are the same. It's important for me to build a method to the madness with routine, so that when I get pushed off the standard track of my role or goals, I can always pivot back quickly. Plus, by using this method I'm less overwhelmed.

I have two important habits that keep me grounded and happy, and boost my productivity:

- I call and spend a lot of time with my family members regularly, no matter where I am in the world. No matter how busy I am. I have learned that family is one of the most important things in life.
- I spend time in nature—this is absolutely essential for me.

The birthday call

In the morning, if I'm making business calls, I always make sure to throw in a call to a mate or associate whose birthday it is. It doesn't have to be long—maybe just a few short minutes—but how great is it to receive a call on your birthday? We take being connected for granted, and so we forget what it means to hear someone's voice we haven't heard in a while. And the enthusiasm behind it! The friendship, the love, the memories... it's a great way to connect.

How we stay connected is as important as being connected in the first place. It's all too easy to send someone an email or instant message, but a letter or phone call is personal and meaningful. Your emotional wellbeing will be that much stronger when you're seeking out and being diligent about keeping these connections.

Sleep

Going to sleep and waking up at a similar time each day is a crucial habit for me. I do my best to go to bed between 10.30 and 11 every night, and to let myself slowly wake up between 4.30 and 5 on weekday mornings (with a sleep-in until 6 am on weekends). In that 30 minutes as I wake up, I visualise the day ahead, thinking through what I've got on, to prepare for it mentally. I sleep with my phone in a different room and don't look at it until 5 am, which is when I see what's happened overnight and how many work emails and texts there are. I also look at the global news and financial markets, and some mornings I give myself some reading time. I'm usually at the gym at 5.20 am, where I finish at 6.20 am, and then I shower and am ready to go by 6.45 am.

Waking up early isn't easy, particularly when days are stressful and tiring. I know how important it is to listen to my body so I give it more rest when needed. I work from home for the first half of every Wednesday (when I am home), and because it's my non-gym day I usually sleep in until 6 am. I then go for a mountain bike ride, or for a walk with my fiancée, or something else fun to start the day. While my team says I'm crazy and vigorous, I allow myself enough time to rest when I'm tired. I listen to my body—my heart has taught me that. But I never ever settle into a different routine. The vibe of being up early and getting on top of key areas in life is so important. I often think that by 9 am high performers have done everyone else's day of work already. Don't waste time.

I'm very deliberate in how I finish each day so that I can easily fall asleep. For someone who's pretty under the pump and always dealing with business pressure and stress, it's pretty remarkable that I don't have problems sleeping. I've learned to deal with stress as best I can, and there is always tomorrow. My routine is to turn off electronics 30 minutes before going to bed because it's proven that screens produce the same ray that the sun does when rising, and you don't want that waking you up just before it's time to sleep. I also make sure that each day is finished well with a list of everything I need to do the next day, which eliminates feelings of overwhelm and helps my mind wind down and relax for sleep. Once my list is written, I switch off. It works a treat every night.

TAKE A MOMENT

- What routine do you currently stick to?
- How do you finish your day so you can easily fall asleep?
- How do you make sure you're getting enough sleep?
- Do you have a wake-up habit?

JOT DOWN YOUR THOUGHTS HERE

Time competes with time

To manage your waking hours effectively, you need to remember that time competes with time. I'm a big auditor of my time, and simply won't waste a minute on bullshit. If I spend an hour with someone or doing something, it's an hour I could have been spending elsewhere. I love spending time on my own and I love being with friends and family, so I'm exceptionally deliberate with each hour of my day. This is because I know what it's like to have nearly died the night before—I know just how precious each second is. I won't let my time be taken up by things that don't deserve it. I live life with a sense of urgency.

Daily break-even analysis

Life is about doing activities that make you feel accomplished and satisfied, so let's take a look at our days in detail to put things into perspective and to break down how we can make the most of every day.

We get 24 hours a day, which is 168 hours in a week, making it 730 hours in a month and 8760 hours in a year. With the average life expectancy around the world being 71.4 years, we would therefore have around 625 464 hours in our lifetime. My experience with my heart at the age of 21 kicked me into gear to closely audit my time, and I refined the skill by learning how my mentors audit their time. Doing so helps them constantly make sure they're ahead of the game and looking after themselves.

TAKE A MOMENT

Here's a breakdown of how I aim to live each day, and how I break it down to help me audit my time more easily. You can use this table to assist in planning your core tasks. Fill in the missing rows to make a total of 24 hours.

DAILY MUSTS WHAT I MUST DO EACH DAY	TIME/AMOUNT
sleep	*6 hours minimum*
reflect	*30 minutes*
meditate	*30 minutes*
move and sweat	*60 minutes minimum*
drink	*4+ litres of water*
	= 24 hours

TAKE A MOMENT

Calculate where you currently spend your time each day using this table and compare this to the table on page 68.

TASK	TOTAL TIME	RELATES TO?	DOES THIS TASK HELP YOU PROSPER?
Assess FY19 budget	*50 min*	*Finance*	*X*

I also make sure that every day I:

- eat fruit and veggies
- say thanks as often as possible
- learn something new
- feel like I've made a difference to a person's life
- feel like I've made a difference to the planet's resources
- scare myself
- feel loved
- have a cuddle with my loved one.

That's what I do my best to live by. When I successfully stick to it, I feel fulfilled and satisfied.

I talk more about this in chapter 8, where I introduce you to my 'Daily Rocks' time management sheet.

Coffee currency

Another way I audit my time is in the way I manage meetings. I don't like messing around or wasting time. My meetings usually take 40 minutes, and if they take an hour they've got to be really serious. My view is that we all know what we need to do, so let's get on with doing it. I encourage my team to be prepared for meetings and to get to the facts straight away: where we are and what we need to do. I don't like meetings that drag on forever, where no-one is offering value and you just wonder when it will end. Hopefully one day soon I won't be doing any formal meetings! My ideal meeting is riding surfboards or mountain bikes while discussing business.

Wherever I can replace a meeting with a coffee, I do; I call it 'coffee currency'. Meeting for coffee can be short and sweet, and you gain just as much as from a formal, sit-down meeting. I can't tell you how many times I've met with potential and current customers, associates, mentors, investors and others for a quick coffee and gained more from that half hour than I could have imagined! It's amazing the number of leads, networking opportunities and potential sales that can come from a simple conversation over coffee—I've generated millions of dollars of deals from it.

Without the formalities of an hour-long meeting the simple act of sitting down for a quick coffee is almost a social wonder: we can small-talk, banter, catch up and 'talk shop'—so to speak—in a rhythm that's more in tune with our busy lifestyles. It's less pressured, more natural, and I find it's more focused. Plus, you can fit more coffee catch-ups into a week than you can long meetings.

Rather than having a full-on, sit-down meeting with staff, I'll say, 'Let's go for a walk and grab a coffee'. That way we get out of the office and move, which puts us in a better state. We get to walk and grab a coffee, which is nice. And we have our discussion in a more personal, real way that's far more fruitful than sitting formally in one of our meeting rooms.

Another great benefit of the coffee catch-up is that most people can fit it into their schedule sooner. Sometimes you might be dealing with a person whose schedule is fully booked for months, and a coffee is all they can manage. It never hurts to ask someone to join you for a cup of coffee.

I call it the coffee *currency* because, just as with our own real-life units of currency, it has no value intrinsically until it is put to work. If you give a dollar to three people, each will have a different idea of its value. It's the same with the coffee date. It might only be 15 minutes, but it's up to you to make those 15 minutes count. Just as you would prepare for a meeting, so too you ought to prepare for the coffee date. And it's this preparation that gives the coffee currency its real value. When you're restricted to only being able to ask two or three questions—or maybe only one—instead of having a long meeting with ample time, it forces you to focus on what's *really* important to discuss.

MICK'S TIPS FOR USING THE COFFEE CURRENCY TO YOUR ADVANTAGE

- During the holidays, everybody is busy. If you can't have lunch with everyone, squeeze in a coffee.
- If you've been eyeing someone who might be an asset to your organisation, invite them for a coffee. This could be a potential employee, board member or freelancer. It's always nice to get a feel for someone informally to see how you click.
- For a potential mentor or business associate—say an investor—weigh up your options. If you can get a formal sit-down, it might be wise to take them up on it, but if there's no time, use your coffee currency and make every moment count.

I once met an early-stage investor (he was an original founder of the video game Call of Duty) at an event. He was notoriously busy and hard to contact. I spoke to him very quickly, and later, with heaps of persistence, eventually managed to secure a 10-minute window to see him. Our 10-minute coffee turned into an hour, and a week later he wrote me a cheque for $100 000. He's been an amazing mentor ever since.

- Remember that when you're wrapped up in your work, the coffee currency can be spent on catching a break with friends or family. This is important, too, and even a few minutes can re-energise you and remind you of why you're working so hard in the first place!
- Make sure you're clear about the purpose of the coffee date and that you prepare beforehand so you can make the 15 to 30 minutes cover everything you need it to.
- Don't waste the other person's time—or yours. Small-talk is fine, but remember the purpose of the catch-up. If you have a question, don't beat around the bush. Ask it.
- If you're meeting a potential employee or business associate, stick to your gut. Pay attention to the little things: how people conduct themselves in public goes a long way to telling you how they will behave later on. If you pay attention, you'll soon develop a good barometer for judging a person's genuineness.

When I registered ONTHEGO® as a trademark I had an issue that would have cost me *tens* of thousands of dollars to fix. So I took a lawyer I knew for coffee, and in an hour he taught me what I needed to do to fight it myself. Through implementing his advice I won the dispute, and ONTHEGO® has become a multimillion-dollar trademark. Plus, I got to learn what IP protection means—and it only cost me a coffee.

Add a touch of healthy pressure

Making your goals happen requires pressure. When you're taking an adventurous path through life that isn't pressured by others, you need to manufacture pressure so you'll still progress quickly. For example, many freelancers or small business owners struggle to hold themselves accountable and consequently don't hustle enough, which means they don't get sufficient work to turn their freelancing into a fulltime gig. If you want to achieve a lot you've got to have pressure, and if there's no external pressure, you need to manufacture it yourself. The reason my successful friends do a lot and achieve a lot is because of the pressure they put on themselves, and I know that the main reason I've been successful is thanks to the pressure I've put on myself. My threshold for handling pressure is really high—in fact, I can only handle life with a lot of pressure; it gives me direction. Without it I'd be lost! It's a weird addiction.

Before we look at adding healthy pressure to your work and life, let's assess the current pressures you're under. What are they? And why are they there? Are they there for a good reason and are they helping you, or are they making you overly stressed and overwhelmed? People put themselves under pressure for dumb things they can't control, like the idea that they need to own a house or be married by a certain age. Why? What's the reason you're pressuring yourself to be married? You can't control when you'll meet the right person. And why the pressure to own your own home? There are other ways to build wealth (which we look at in chapter 9). Another unhealthy pressure is social media. People feel like they have to look a certain way and have a cool-looking life online, but that unhealthy pressure is stupid, painful and counterproductive.

To use pressure well you need to know how much you can handle. Some people put too much pressure on themselves and burn out, which is counterproductive. The whole point of pressuring yourself is to help you achieve your goals, so as soon as it becomes too much you need to pull back. Make sure you check in regularly: am I putting too much pressure on myself? Is this good pressure or bad pressure? Gear the pressure up and down according to your capacity: do I need to refresh myself or ramp it up?

And don't be afraid to heat up the pressure regularly. It can become addictive!

TAKE A MOMENT

Are you giving in to dumb pressures? Have a good think, and mentally get rid of every pressure that isn't helping you, or that's out of your control. Doing this will free up mental and emotional space for healthy, productive pressures.

What type of pressures do you have? Which ones are productive?

JOT DOWN YOUR THOUGHTS HERE

ROUNDUP

- Learning is not only challenging, engaging and fun—it's empowering and humbling, so try to learn something new every day.
- Habits such as spending time with your family and in nature will keep you grounded and happy.
- A strict, regular sleep routine is a must if you want to stay on top of your game.
- Being deliberate with each hour of your day will prevent you from losing precious time. Remember: time competes with time.
- Using 'coffee currency' is a great substitute for unnecessarily long meetings.
- Creating healthy pressure on yourself will give you direction and help you achieve your goals.

IF YOU DON'T CHANGE ANYTHING IN YOUR LIFE FOR A PERIOD OF TIME, YOU GET STUCK

FOCUS ON MAKING CHANGES WEEK TO WEEK

CHAPTER 6

BE BOLD ABOUT YOUR PERSONAL VISION

When there's something you're passionate about getting done, you've got to be bold and share your vision. Whether it's a side project, an initiative at the office, a career advancement or a business, you've got to be vocal about it. You want everyone around you to catch your enthusiasm and to want to help you, even if it's just in minor ways. External help can make a big difference. If you're generally shy, focus on showing your passion for what you're working on and people will be drawn to you.

When I was washing windows as a kid I approached strangers nonstop, enthusiastically helping them carry their shopping bags and asking if they wanted their windows cleaned. I would have had zero customers if I hadn't been bold. Likewise, when I began OTG I couldn't stop talking about it! It was—and still is—my baby. How do first-time parents react when you ask about their child? They gush and shower you with pictures! They tell you how beautiful and perfect the baby is, and how he or she is developing. You want to do the same with what you're working on.

Self-promote

We all are a brand. Whether you're building a company, a charity or your career, people will judge what you're doing and the value of it. Promoting yourself, your cause, your path or your start-up is one of the most important things you can do to grow it without the traditional means of massive advertising. Hands down, self-promotion can make or break your endeavour in the beginning. It's vital to positively self-promote wherever possible. As Richard Branson says, the best ambassador of your cause is you!

I'm often referred to as a self-promoter; it always came naturally to me. Maybe because I have insecurities that make me want everyone to know what I'm doing, and to see my hardships and growth in order to inspire them. I know it doesn't come naturally for everybody, but everything is a learnable skill (there are many, many things that didn't come naturally to me that I've had to learn!).

Self-promotion is not pounding your chest and saying, 'Here I am!' and 'Look at me!' It's easy to confuse it with that behaviour, but for me self-promotion means being positive about what I'm doing, and from that positive feeling I follow the natural desire to share it with the world at every appropriate moment. Think about it: when you found that person who made your heart beat faster, didn't you want to share them with the rest of the world? Or when you discovered some latent talent inside yourself? Or perhaps when someone helped you out, didn't you want to praise their work to the world?

We're social creatures. Sharing is not only good for us, it can also be interesting and inspiring for others. Great self-promotion can be as simple as sharing what you do, with passion and energy, to a taxi driver. You never know what might come of it! In 2015 OTG had been operating for three years. I was in a taxi in Hong Kong, and I got chatting to the driver. He was from Pakistan and he was interested to learn more about OTG because, as it turned out, his brother was running a substantial factory in Pakistan. He introduced me to his brother, and today his is still one of our biggest factories. Incredible!

I've met many people in hotel lobbies, on planes, and simply out and about who have become customers. In fact, I recently met someone in a hotel lobby who is on the board of the Australian National Basketball League (NBL), and we got chatting. Since that initial chat, he has introduced me to the owner of the NBL. My general manager, Caggi, and I recently met him and his son on their multimillion-dollar private yacht. We were pinching ourselves walking onto the yacht. Now, OTG is making some training and playing apparel for the NBL. The lesson there is: you never know where your next major client, mentor or friend will come from. Get out there and promote yourself and be confident to talk to anyone.

Be coachable

Part of being bold is being coachable. You need to be bold not only in your actions, but in how much you seek feedback and opportunities for growth. It's important that we acknowledge that we actually don't know much, and that we have *heaps* to learn. I certainly didn't know much, but I was coachable. We sometimes mistakenly think that 'successful' people have it all figured out, but that's not the case at all. Most people who have made a name for themselves in their chosen field are as knowledgeable as they are because they sought, and still seek, coaching from those who know more than they do. Nobody who is successful today was successful when they began (and most weren't even successful after five years, 10 years or more!). Being coachable is not only about seeking out coaching; it's also about listening to feedback when you haven't asked for it. If you have people in your life willing to confront you on things you've done, or ways you've communicated, and who show you how you could have done it better, that's special. Rather than getting offended and upset, give them a massive hug! They just helped you on your journey of their own volition.

Believe passionately

To successfully promote yourself you need to believe, wholeheartedly, in what you're doing. Jeff Bezos of Amazon believed firmly that people would buy books online and that he could offer them more cheaply than their bricks-and-mortar counterparts. Starbucks chairman and CEO Howard Schultz believed that premium coffee could be sold in franchises. Steve Jobs of Apple believed passionately that the average person would utilise computing power to their advantage, in their own home, each and every day. My team at OTG is extremely supportive of me because they believe in my abilities and see real progress. My investors and stakeholders in the company are passionate about me being the face of OTG because they see someone who believes firmly in what he's doing. It's super important you believe wholeheartedly in your vision.

If reading this has made you realise you don't believe passionately in what you're doing or in your vision, then move on and find something you can get behind 100 per cent.

Change it up

There's a fabled experiment about five monkeys in an enclosure that has a ladder with a banana at the top of it. When the monkeys run up the ladder to get the banana they are sprayed with water, which they dislike, and they quickly learn not to go for the banana. One monkey is then taken out of the enclosure and a new one is put in. It immediately runs up the ladder to get the banana, only to be pulled back by the others. Then another monkey is taken out and replaced, until all five monkeys in the enclosure have never actually experienced the water being sprayed, yet they all still avoid the banana and stop newcomers from climbing the ladder.

How often do we do things just because we always have, without re-examining why? I see change as a good thing. A *very* good thing. And it's something you must instil in your life if you want to grow and evolve. It's important to change things up regularly: to really examine why you're doing things, and whether it still makes sense to do them. Is that habit of drinks every Friday night helping you get where you want to go? Is it time to try Coles Delivery so you can go for a walk rather than do the grocery shopping? The small things count.

Actively do things that will make you see life through a new, different lens. Whether that's travelling, enjoying books, documentaries, or movies from other cultures or perspectives, putting your hand up for different tasks at work, or applying for new roles to broaden or deepen your skillset, have an attitude of changing things up and it will help move your career forward.

When I took on my first big order for the 400 cycling jerseys it was a massive change, and the rush of being so far in the deep end became an addiction. It was all new and different and exciting.

I've since built the habit of constantly thinking, 'I've got to change; don't get too comfortable, Mick'. If you don't change anything in your life for a period of time, you get stuck. Focus on making changes week to week. Not necessarily big changes—small iterations of change are powerful. Maybe spend less on clothes, or go away one weekend a month, or take lessons to learn a new language. You could start by doing something once a month that you know is going to scare you a bit. Something that'll keep you on your toes. Something different. Whatever works best for you, build the regular habit of changing things up.

Learn to network

At school I could barely see the blackboard, but I didn't want to be 'that guy' sitting up front. Who does at that age? So in high school I identified who the smart kids were and asked them to explain the concepts we had just been taught in class, in their own words. Some of my classmates were willing to lend me their notes, which helped even further. This early foundation in networking, and not being afraid to ask people for advice, has helped me tremendously. My sister, Alicia, calls it my 'fearless capability'!

Part of the importance of promoting yourself and passionately sharing what you're up to at every appropriate opportunity is how it can build your network. There's a great book called *Never Eat Alone* by Keith Ferrazzi that talks about the power of networking to propel your career forward. The saying, 'it's not what you know, it's who you know' still applies today. Yes, you need to know your stuff. But unless you know people who can introduce you to people who can mentor you, or refer your work, or offer you a job, it'll take much longer for you to get where you want to go.

In the early days I networked like mad to make sales, and it worked really well. I'd go to a lot of networking events where I was located, and as I progressed in the business I started travelling farther to go to events more specific to my industry.

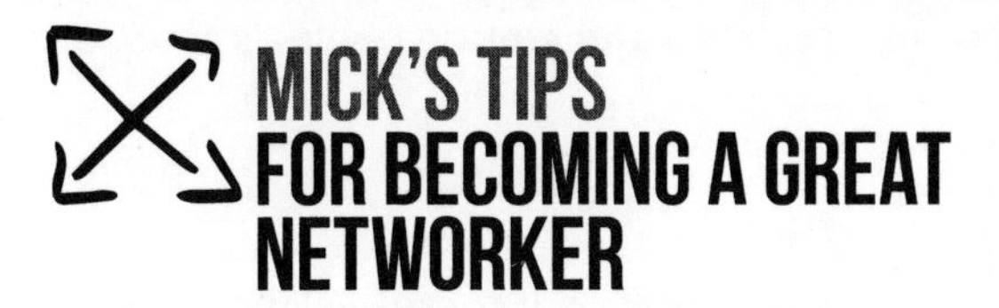

MICK'S TIPS FOR BECOMING A GREAT NETWORKER

Follow these tips and you'll be networking in no time.

Have a networking strategy

Network constantly, but be strategic about it. In my early days I went to every free networking event I could find, to meet new people. I would make sure that by the end of the night I had met at least 80 per cent of the people in the room. If possible, find out who's going to be there ahead of time—who is most important to meet—and think deeply about what you want to get out of the event.

Be interested in others—it's not all about you

Don't talk about yourself when you meet people; ask them about themselves. You don't want to do the straight introduction and a hard sell—you want to build the relationship. Start by finding out what you have in common—maybe it's a sport, a hobby or a common interest. And then keep it in mind for future reference. For example, Steve loves rugby, Anna is nuts for health food, Robert loves science fiction movies. If you have to write

(continued)

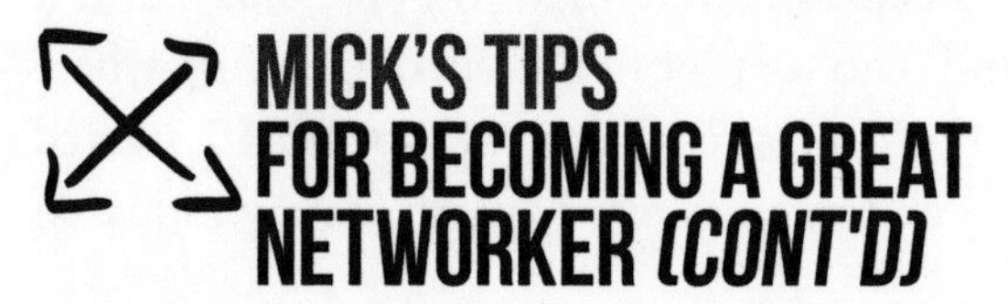

these down, do it. If you're naturally a people person then it might be second nature to remember people's unique interests.

Sell softly

There are a lot of ugly networkers out there—slimy people who just try and sell. Don't be one of them. It's all about finding people's passions and problems. Listen more. Take notes, and remember facts.

Be efficient

Don't go to every single networking event if the same people are going to be attending. I'd go to networking events in my home town, but never back to the same ones because the same people, with whom I'd already built relationships, would have been there. Go to one event, dominate it, build good relationships out of it, and then go to another, dominate it, and repeat. I remember Paul Zahra, former CEO and managing director of David Jones (a $2+ billion department store chain in Australia), who mentored me for some time, saying, 'Always be the first one there, and the first to leave'. Get there first, make a strong impression, make progress quickly and leave early to move on to your other important tasks and meetings.

Follow up

After each networking event I'd go home, put every business card on my desk, and write emails to everyone that night. I wanted to make the biggest impact possible, and I wanted them to remember me. For example:

> Hey Andrew,
>
> It was great to catch up with you tonight. You're doing amazing work. I'd love to keep in touch.
>
> By the way, if your organisation ever needs uniforms, let's catch up for a coffee. I'd love to chat.
>
> Cheers,
>
> Mick

I had CEOs writing back to me saying, 'Thanks mate. I really appreciated meeting you as well. Let's keep in touch'. I generated a lot of business from doing this! It's not all about the short-term gains.

Another way to follow up is to ask the event organiser for a list of who went to the event—they don't always give this out, but when they do it's a great list to have.

Understand the boundaries

There are boundaries in every relationship. Be decent and appropriate, professional and personable, and treat people well. Don't ask for too much, and don't give your heart and soul to help others while receiving nothing in return.

Back it up

The essential ingredient of self-promotion is being able to back up what you say. You have to walk your talk. If you're passionately sharing how your endeavour is changing things, make sure you're able to demonstrate what and how you're changing things. Self-promotion isn't just talk: it's talk about real action and results you're achieving. People want to see progress: to build trust in your cause. Often there are too many 'get rich quick' schemes or 'wannabeprenuers'. Be real. One currency you can't get back is respect. Show people what your initiative looks like in action. Show them the culture behind the brand. Show them how you're getting stakeholders on board at the office to change things. Show them your failures and your results after learning those hard lessons. Back up your vision with results.

Ignore the naysayers

Naysayers. We all come across them, and we've all been one at some stage. There will always be some naysayers who talk you down—there's no way around it. The only thing in your control is whether you listen to what they say or not, whether you let it affect you or not, and how you build your network of supportive people who do have your back. My mentor Hap Klopp (founder of The North Face) told me that 'as an entrepreneur, more people will *misunderstand* you than *understand* you. Just get used to it'. He was spot on. I'm constantly misunderstood by people who don't personally know me, sometimes in a good way and often in a bad way, but I've gotten used to it. I don't let it affect me.

Naysayers are typically pretty unhappy with their lives; often the first thing they'll say is, 'Well he's showing off a bit, isn't he?'

What happy, fulfilled, purpose-driven person ever felt the need to talk negatively about someone else? People's negative words might be a jealous response to you having figured things out and building your dream. They're oblivious to the stress you live with, unaware of the hours you spend working while they're hanging out with friends at the bar, or playing PlayStation, or travelling on holidays. The first three years that I ran my business, no-one knew me. I was working seven days a week. I had no money. It was a tough slog, but I could see what we were building and I loved it. Only now is OTG becoming well known. As the saying goes, it takes five to 10 years to become an 'overnight' success. Block out the naysayers and keep working on what makes your heart come alive. In Dr Seuss's words, 'Those who matter don't mind, and those who mind don't matter'.

When I started OTG, pretty much none of my friends at the time understood why, and they thought I was stupid. Why would someone drop out of university to pursue building a business with absolutely no capital in a horrible economy? They said, 'Why don't you go work with your dad's building company?', or 'Why don't you finish your uni degree and then do something?' It didn't make sense to them, and so none of them supported me. I lost a lot of friends due to their lack of understanding and support, which made it a lonely journey. But on the way I've found many new friends who are there for me, and I am there for them.

As I've gotten older and have experienced countless naysayers, I've found that I care less and less about what people think of me. Ratan Tata says it perfectly: 'Take the stones people throw at you and use them to build a monument'. Today I only care what the people I respect, and who are important to me, think. It's freeing. You are your environment, so be careful of the energy around you.

The tall poppy syndrome

In Australia we have what's referred to as 'tall poppy syndrome', which is when successful people are resented, attacked, cut down and criticised because of their success and progress in their chosen field. We've typically been a society that wants everyone to be on the same, equal level. The positive side of this is that we're hugely supportive of the underdog, and we rally together and help each other in the aftermath of a crisis or natural disaster like nowhere else. We have a great sense of mateship: of helping a mate (who is often a stranger) out. The negative side of this desire to be on the same level is that we cut down anyone who tries to be a bit too successful, a bit too innovative, a bit too clever or a bit too rich. Things are changing with the rise of the 'hustle' attitude or 'entrepreneur' career, but there's still a way to go before there will be acceptance of achiever peers. As I've achieved more and more, I've had people shoot me down more and more. It's why my daily habits are so important—they keep me centred and balanced. People will often see the publicity, the awards, the contract winnings, the investment deals or networking I've done (which, mind you, I never thought I would have!). What they don't see or don't think about is the times of stress and worry, not knowing how I'm going to get a project completed. The stress on a Friday night about cash flow. The 12- to 18-hour-long days, including travel. The friends and family members' birthdays I've missed out on. Going to buy basic groceries hoping my debit card has enough funds on it, waiting in anticipation for an 'approved' or 'declined'. The multiple weeks and years I worked with no break. Some call it 'living life on the edge'. My brother, Nathan, once said, 'People misunderstand Mick's enthusiasm and what he was doing in the early years. They mistake it for jealousy and bragging. And I stick it to them now. When I'm hanging around in a new Aston Martin my brother just bought, I make sure they get a text'.

Being shot down and judged negatively again and again doesn't feel nice. We all have that fear of judgement. Laurence Olivier, a famous English actor who was universally lauded, said that stage fright is 'always waiting outside the door, waiting to get you. You either battle or walk away'. He feared being judged constantly throughout his career. We all experience that fear, no matter our personality or upbringing, or our level of 'success'. We're all unsure of ourselves at times. The goal is to not let that fear stop you from taking action: focus on what's important to you. Remind yourself *why* you're doing what you're doing. And don't refrain from talking about your progress—just be real, humble and down-to-earth when you share what you're achieving. Remember that what you have to offer can bring good not only to you but to others, through employment, through charity, or through a product or service that's exceptional. People won't stop talking about you, and that's fine.

Self-promotion never ends

In today's world, if you want cut-through, self-promotion never ends. The story you passionately share will change as you progress, your industry will change over the years and in business your customers' expectations will change. But through your whole journey you need to keep self-promoting. We're in an age where anyone can become an expert in their field quickly. With social channels and the internet, we can reach literally anyone. Be ready to answer questions enthusiastically. And sometimes it'll be tough. You're totally exhausted when you bump into someone who wants to talk to you about what you're doing, and you have to dig deep to find the energy to be present and engaged with them. Put in that extra effort and you'll be amazed at what comes out of it. Believing in your brand (personal or business), owning your story, guarding your reputation and learning how to communicate it with others always reaps rewards. So take risks; knock on doors; keep self-promoting.

Promote, but be wise on social media

Social media is a tool that can further your personal brand and your career. We're fortunate today that we have tools to spread our message far and wide; the barriers to connecting with people are dropping, and you can use that to your advantage.

When used effectively, social media can be very powerful in bringing momentum and growth to what you're working on. However, it can also be dangerous. It affects people's emotional state, in some cases with severe consequences. Photoshopped images shared on social media inspire deep insecurities in some viewers, even causing eating disorders for some. There are cases of people becoming depressed from viewing other people's 'perfect' lives online, and feeling inadequate in comparison. They forget that what people share online is unrealistic and edited, only showing the happy, good moments; only showing the successes, not all the moments of disappointment and setbacks.

The other negative side of social media is the distraction it brings. People waste an insane amount of precious time scrolling endlessly. It's hard to become the best version of yourself when your mind is cluttered by everyone's filtered life on social media. So use social media for your benefit, and be wary of its negative effects on your life.

Social media do's and don'ts

The first thing people do is search your name. What do you look like if someone searches you on Google or opens your Facebook profile? Before anyone works with anyone, they do some research online. This happens in recruitment too! Employers are hiring on the basis of what people look like on social media, so make sure you look good. If you're behind a cause (like your own business), use it to its advantage and make sure you come across exactly as you want your personal brand portrayed.

Social media can be your best friend and your worst enemy. Here's how to make it work in your favour.

First impressions

Make sure you have a great photo of yourself—not necessarily a professional headshot, but something you would be happy with a potential employer, mentor, investor or customer seeing. Add a captivating bio statement saying who you are, what you love doing and your vision of where you're going.

(continued)

Consistency

Make sure your branding (including photos and bios) is consistent across all social media platforms.

Be calculated

Make sure you're only sharing things you're happy with the whole world seeing. Nothing is gated on social media; people can get access to everything. If you have some old posts you don't want important people to see, delete them.

Spend time thinking through what your niche offering in your role is, or what your most important beliefs and passions are that you want to become a thought leader around. Social media is a great tool to get awareness around these, and to build up your personal brand.

Post regularly

Social media is a machine that works best when it's constantly fed. If you're posting a few times a day, getting comments and replying, you'll have wider reach. Be sure to monitor your engagement because you don't want to get into the routine of over-posting. Facebook and Instagram now have very smart algorithms that will punish you if you're not being 'smart'.

Have specific social media time

It's important to block out the specific times you'll use social media so you don't become consumed, scrolling through endlessly. Build a habit of when you do (and when you *don't*) use social media so you don't end up wasting precious time on it. Decide when your specific time will be—for example, it could be every time you're waiting in a line—and make sure that you don't go on social media at any other time (and turn off notifications!).

Remember: it's all edited

Remember that everything you see online has been edited; it's never the full story. The photos are edited, what people say is edited to show a specific side of themselves, and what people choose to not say is edited. We never see the full picture. It's easy to get bogged down thinking that everyone else has it good. They don't. Trust me. Take it all with a grain of salt.

Remember: it's not creating deep relationships

Social media is not the place to create real connection. It's very easy to connect with others and talk to them, which is great, but nothing ever connects you with someone like having a coffee, or going for a walk together. That's how supportive and enduring relationships are built. Be on top of this as there are certainly risks for the human brain in today's digital world.

It's easy for social media to become your enemy, both professionally and personally. This handy table (overleaf) will help you make it your friend.

(continued)

MICK'S TIPS FOR USING SOCIAL MEDIA TO YOUR BENEFIT *(CONT'D)*

DO	DON'T
Know your audience One of the keys to having a social media account that will thrive, whether it's your own personal page or one for your business, is knowing your audience. What are they interested in? What do they want to see and read? How can your social media account provide benefit to them? If you know the answers to these questions then you are on the way to running an engaging and successful account.	*Go for long periods without posting* Think about how many times you have unfollowed an account, not because you don't love the brand or person behind it, but simply because they don't post enough to be worthwhile following. If you want to continue to build your social media presence and brand awareness, make sure you upload to social media a couple of times a week at the very least.
Be active without being over the top If you want to continually increase your social media platform's likes and engagement, then it is crucial to upload quality content on a regular basis. Nobody is interested in following a ghost account with occasional, erratic uploads. Be consistent with your posting, but keep in mind that your followers don't want to be spammed either.	*Ignore comments and DMs* If people are leaving comments and DMs, it means they are interested in what you have to offer. Don't ignore this! Thank them by replying. This will encourage them to continue engaging with your future content.

DO	DON'T
Maintain a regular look and feel and tone of voice If you want your message to be clear, make sure you maintain your own unique look and feel across all imagery that goes out on your social media platforms. This is the same with your tone of voice. Your followers should be able to immediately recognise you through your images and tone of voice.	*Post anything you don't want the world to know about* You need to be comfortable with absolutely anyone seeing everything you post on social media. While you can hide posts from certain people, or even delete the post after a period of time, don't forget that screenshots last forever! Never upload something if you aren't happy with everyone seeing it.
Be creative and push boundaries While it's crucial to stay within your look, feel and tone of voice, don't forget to be creative! After all, if you think of some of your favourite accounts, they all push the boundaries and showcase creative content by thinking outside the box. Don't be afraid to push the boundaries with your content every now and then.	*Buy followers* When you buy followers, you are just buying a number. These 'followers' aren't really interested in following you, and they will provide 0% engagement. Therefore, there is going to be a huge discrepancy between the number of followers on your account and the number of likes on your posts. This isn't the only negative. Purchasing followers violates most platforms' Terms of Service. If they notice you have been doing this, you are eventually going to have your account removed.

(continued)

DO	DON'T
Choose positivity over negativity	*Choose quantity over quality*
Positive news receives better reach and engagement on social media than negative news does. Therefore, use this to your advantage! If you have something fun or exciting going on, take a snap and share it across your channels. Don't hold back from spreading the positivity across your channel!	While it's important to regularly engage your followers with new content, make sure you don't start uploading content that isn't to an excellent standard. Always put the quality of your posts first. In the grand scheme of things, your followers aren't going to notice if you miss an upload day, but they will start to disengage if your quality starts to drop.

ROUNDUP

- Never stop promoting yourself or your brand: be positive about what you're doing and share it with the world with passion and energy, but not in a boastful way.
- Being coachable is about listening to feedback even when you haven't asked for it. Be grateful for what this teaches you and don't be offended or upset.
- Believe passionately in what you're doing and follow your vision wholeheartedly. If you don't feel you can do that, move on to something that you can get behind 100 per cent.
- Change things up regularly and see change as a good thing. Even small changes can make a big difference if you want to grow and evolve.
- Learn to network—a lot of the time it's not what you know, it's who you know.
- You have to walk your talk, so ensure you can back up any claims that you make.
- Don't let naysayers get you down. Ignore them, be bold and pursue your vision.
- Never let fear stop you from taking action: focus on what's important to you and keep reminding yourself *why* you're doing what you're doing.
- Beware of how you use social media. It can further your personal brand or ruin your career.

WHEN YOU'RE CONFRONTED WIT

MASSIV

NEW CHALLENG

YOUR NETWORK O

SUPPORTIV

DEPENDABL

GREAT PEOPL

IS YOUR

PARACHUT

CHAPTER 7

HARD-HITTING TRUTHS

Let's dive a bit deeper into what it takes to live a big, meaningful life. Some of what we cover in this chapter may challenge you, or you may have resistance to really taking on board what I'm saying. Do your best to embrace it. Yes, it might be outside of your comfort zone, but trust me, I know what that feels like. I intimately know that initial feeling of fear, that lack of confidence, that thought: 'Can I really do this?' It's totally fine to have that thought; what isn't fine is to let that thought dictate your actions. *You* want to dictate your actions. *You* want to be in charge of your life.

Let's start by looking at the kind of smarts you need to be successful. If you do nothing else but focus on these six principles, you'll go a long way.

The smarts you need (and they're not what you think)

I wasn't an A student by any means, but I was determined to not be stupid. One of the many things that paralyse us in the pursuit of our goals is thinking that we're not smart enough to achieve them. The self-doubt, the worry that we can't compete and believing that others are smarter than us can be crippling. But remember: we're all smart at what we're smart at.

Steve Jobs said, 'The world is full of people no smarter than you and I'. People usually think that being smart is about being clever, nerdy or really good at maths. It certainly can be those things, but being smart is about much more than that: it's about the decision-making process. Don't worry about what grades you did or didn't get in school or at uni (remember, I got 44 per cent in year 12 and I dropped out of uni), and instead focus on six principles: be informed, be selective, be open, be determined, be committed and never stop learning. That's all the smarts you need to excel.

Be informed

Make informed decisions. It only takes a small bit of extra effort to research and understand something more than you did before, so take the time out of your day to inform yourself about what you're pursuing. Study daily, even if only for 10 minutes, and take notes. Never underestimate the amount of education available online through peer to peer. The more you know, the smarter the decisions you will be able to make. Remember that after 10 000 hours of doing one thing, you're considered an expert. This doesn't require a genius level IQ—it requires continually working at the same thing.

Be selective

Be very selective when it comes to your time, and your money. The smartest people are those who manage their time and money the best. Being selective also means learning how to say 'no' to people and projects that would take you off course, which isn't always easy, but it's important to learn how to do it kindly and firmly. Remember the 80/20 rule: 80 per cent of your results come from 20 per cent of your actions. Identify what those actions are and focus on more of those.

Be open

Being selective doesn't mean that you can no longer be open to new things, ideas or people. In fact, the more selective you are, the more you'll be able to weed out the good from the bad, and you'll find yourself being more open to the new. Know and accept that the path to your goals will be new and uncertain, with unknown obstacles. When you're open, you'll discover new ways to get past challenges and continue moving forward. It's so important to be open.

Richard Branson once told me a story. He was running late for a meeting and the taxi driver who picked him up was begging him to listen to a music tape of his because he knew Virgin was involved in recording music. Branson was anxious, and worst of all the driver had left the tape at his mother's place. The driver persuaded Branson to allow him to drive to the meeting destination via his mother's house to listen to the tape. After a much longer than expected trip, Branson listened to the tape and was so impressed with the song that he agreed to meet the driver again at Virgin Records. That driver was Phil Collins, and that song was 'In the Air Tonight', which went on to become one of Virgin's best-selling records!

You never know who you'll meet—at what train station or beach, at what time of day—who may just change your life forever. That's real.

Be determined

Determination means being focused on your goal, and having it in mind at all times. Be determined to achieve it, and utilise every moment to help you on your mission. For example, when others are watching TV to chill, you're watching it for information. What kind of brand is this? What kind of new market is opening up? What demographics are watching this show now? It also means the path of your learning changes so the outcomes you require are the pieces of information you seek.

Be committed

Being committed means sticking to your cause and belief. Even when things are tough. It means designing your daily habits to support you for optimum performance—to be grounded and pumped, so that when challenges arise you're instantly brainstorming how to move past them, rather than letting them get to you. Being committed is what takes you from a smart strategy with great potential to awesome reality.

Never stop learning

It's essential to have an attitude of continuous learning; there's always something you can learn, from everybody. Every day, focus on listening more than you talk, and see everything as an opportunity to learn. Ask questions. Be inquisitive.

Fake it

When you need to fake it, it means you're pushing the boundaries, which is how you achieve more than you previously thought you'd be able to. Through almost every step of my business I've been in the deep end, under pressure. I've constantly started before I was ready, faking it until I made it, pulling it all together as I went along. It's still the way I love to do business! The only way to progress to the next level is to look like you're already there. I'm not the only one who does this. I've met people running massive businesses and people in really big corporate jobs who are still faking it in some ways, and for good reason. It helps build the future. I've never bitten off more than I could chew—though my tolerance for chewing a lot at once is pretty high!

OTG recently signed a million-dollar contract with a professional English football league team to make all the players' outfits, on and off the field, as well as all the fan retail merchandise. It was a full suite of products, which we'd never done before, and we had a 6- to 10-week turnaround time on around 90000 units. I knew we could pull it off, but it was definitely pushing the limits. The football league was used to dealing with massive, multimultimillion-dollar companies, so we had to act like we were one. We faked it, and we backed it up and delivered all the goods on time and to specification; it was a big leap forward for us. You'd be surprised by what you can pull off! Sir Richard Branson said, 'If somebody offers you an amazing opportunity but you are not sure you can do it, say yes—then learn how to do it later!'

Build your parachute

Once you have your vision for your future and know the work you want to do, it's important to actively create a network of people who will support you through thick and thin. The inner turmoil that comes with embarking on a new endeavour can make or break you. It's a battle between what you think (and hope) you can do and what you believe you can't do. You need good people who believe in you to abate your fears, and to remind you what you're made of. There will be a lot of naysayers who talk you down, and though it's usually a product of their own fear and anxiety, it can bring you down at times. Again, this is when you will need those good people around you—you need to be in the right environment to reach your goals. In fact, sometimes the only thing that holds people back is their unsupportive environment.

If someone is not empowering you, they're not helping you become the best version of yourself. Don't take it personally, and remember that it's okay to move away from those kinds of people. If you have a network of people around you who don't believe in you and what you can do—who don't 'get it'—then taking a leap will be 10 times harder. You must audit your network. Walking away from unsupportive people doesn't mean it's the end of the relationship. Sometimes you'll reconnect a few years later and be able to have a great, supportive friendship again. Always stay open-ended with that possibility for the future. Business philosopher Jim Rohn famously said, 'You are the average of the five people you spend the most time with'.

I like the analogy of picturing myself in the belly of an aeroplane, ready to jump. The hatch is open, the wind is blowing in my face and I put on my goggles. Almost ready to jump, I reach back to see if my parachute's on because that parachute is my lifeline. Would you jump without a parachute? In work and in life, when you're confronted with a massive new challenge, your network of supportive, dependable, great people is your parachute. You can get on the plane, you can even fly up to a high altitude, but don't jump before you have that network.

Hard conversations

Having hard conversations is a part of life. Sometimes there's good news to share, and sometimes there are tricky, awkward things that have to be shared. Hard conversations typically happen when you quit your job, ask for a pay rise, need to fire someone, decide to break up with your boyfriend or girlfriend, have to tell your landlord you're moving out, have to tell someone you can't pay them back in time, need to break it to someone that they piss you off, and more.

One of the best strategies I've learned for dealing with hard conversations came from my chairman: 'Tell good news fast, and bad news faster'. I use it all the time, and it's helped me get through a lot of hard conversations. When it's bad news, cut to the chase. Trying to soften the blow can extend the hard conversation further than necessary. Of course, you always want to say it nicely. Always. Just don't beat around the bush. It's like a bandaid: rip it off!

When you need to have a hard conversation with someone, make sure it's in person. Never cop out and do it over text message, Facebook messenger, or email. That's bad taste and negatively affects your long-term relationship. Face it, share it in person, be nice and be fast.

Another strategy that makes hard conversations easier is to set proper expectations in the beginning, before it gets hard. Before you enter into a commitment with someone—whether a boss, mentor, landlord or crush—have a conversation about the end. I know it's not hugely romantic, but setting expectations well at the beginning is the best way to make what would be hard conversations much easier. For example, you can say, 'I'm really excited about this opportunity. I think we'll work well together. Let's get started on this with a kind of probation, and review it together in a month to see how we're going and how we're both feeling'. If it's a conversation with a potential boss or employee, discuss salary expectations, and more, upfront.

I've had to have many hard conversations in running OTG. There have been times when I've had to let people go because I knew it was the right time for them to move on, and it's been tough. During the course of working together, we've become close friends, and now I've got to sit them down and say they're being let go. 'I don't think it's right for you, or for us, to continue moving forward. You're not going to become the best version of yourself here.' Saying it like it is—showing them I care about them and their own development and career, and facing the reality by having that hard conversation with them—has been essential for both parties.

TAKE A MOMENT

Are there any hard conversations that you've been avoiding? Maybe you need to let your boss know about something sensitive, or let a stakeholder know a project will be delayed. Or maybe it's long overdue for you and your spouse to talk about finances, or about each other's love of languages, or to resolve that fight from three months ago.

Whatever it is that you've been avoiding, pluck up the courage and have the hard conversation. You might be pleasantly surprised at how easy it is! When you're coming from a place of honesty, and you do it in person and cut to the chase, it's a nicer experience for both of you.

JOT DOWN YOUR THOUGHTS HERE

You're not in sales? Think again.

We're constantly selling ourselves; it's not just salespeople who need to sell. In employment we need to sell our ideas, get backing for initiatives, sell ourselves to get a pay rise, and so on. As an entrepreneur you're selling non-stop. As a parent you're selling ideas, behaviours, and better decisions and life strategies to your children. As a spouse you need to sell constantly to get your own way, right? So what is selling?

Let's say the world is ending—it's about to explode, and Richard Branson has a rocket ship, but he's only got one seat left. You have two minutes to tell him why you should get that seat. People often think selling means a pitch like this:

'I've achieved X and Y. I'm a positive person. I'm young. I've got great ideas and know how to execute. I'd be a great addition to your team.'

But this isn't a very good sales pitch. Instead, you could say:

'Richard, I know you're going into space and you're not coming back. Where are the gaps on your team? What don't you have to successfully live in outer space?'

'We have all the engineers and technicians we need, sorry.'

'Okay, and how are you planning to eat? Do you have a chef, someone to cook for everyone and organise meal plans?'

'Well, actually, we don't have a chef…'

'Cool. Hi, my name's Mick and I'm a trained chef. I'd love to complete your team so we can survive out there.'

Selling is about asking questions to find out the problems people have, and then listening to their answers. From there, find the win–win. No matter how innovative and amazing a product, service, idea or strategy is, if it's not what the other person is looking for, there's no sale. The art of the sell is to build a relationship and find out the other party's needs. And remember: sometimes people won't buy what you do, they'll buy why you do it and who you are.

Learn to negotiate

You need to learn how to negotiate. Everything is up for negotiation! Whether it's asking for an upgrade on a plane, to have a deadline extended, to get a pay rise because of the results you've achieved, or to negotiate a better deal for a product or service. We negotiate every day of our lives: with our partners, co-workers, the guy at the car wash. We're giving offers and making counteroffers, all the while trying to better our interests through the process. Think about discussing chores with your partner, or having banter about what's the 'right' way to put on the roll of toilet paper—whose way gets picked? It's all negotiation. When both parties feel they're treated fairly, a relationship can flourish.

Know what you want

To negotiate well and close a good deal you need to know exactly what you want out of it before you enter the negotiation—make sure you're really clear on this. For

(continued)

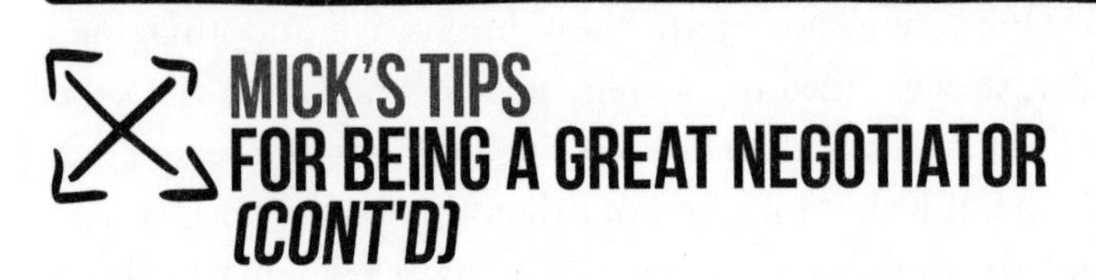

example, when negotiating with a new employer, know exactly what income you want to be earning, whether you want flexible hours two days a week, or to work four days a week so you can work on your own projects on the side.

Find out what is success for them

Do your best to have a good understanding of what success is for the other party, so that you can negotiate in a way that they get what means the most to them, and so they're willing to acquiesce on what means the most to you.

Set the tone

Set the tone at the start of the meeting. Why are we here, and what do we want out of being here?

Pay attention

I recently took my car to the car wash, and this is how my conversation with the attendant went:

'Mick,' he said, 'I can give you a full wash, top of the line, for $60, and you get a free wash for your fiancée's car.'

I thought it sounded pretty good. It was the regular price for the top wash and, on top of it, I would get a free wash for my girlfriend's car.

'Tell you what', he said. 'I've got something for you. This car looks good and it's new. You want to keep it looking great. How about a polish? $150. Twenty-five per cent off the regular price. You get the polish, the wash for your car, and a free wash for your fiancée's car. Can't beat it.'

I thought that sounded even better. It was a discount on the polish because I would be getting the top of the line wash.

'All right', I agreed.

When I went to pay I saw that I was actually paying full price for the polish, and that I got a discounted wash and a free wash for my girlfriend's car. But the polish, which was full price, was the most expensive part. They won, and I lost. I had made a quick assumption when I should have paid attention and asked, 'What, exactly, are you giving me at a discount?' In negotiations, whether at the car wash or at work, you need to give it your full attention so you don't get fooled.

Listen

Make sure you're always listening more than talking. Being quiet and letting the other person speak more means the words you do say can be *bang on* to the point.

Be reasonable

You're always looking for a win–win; you're not trying to negotiate it so that you win and they lose. That's not nice. Negotiating isn't about making outlandish asks. It's about two parties going back and forth until both are happy. You don't want to come across as too tough a negotiator. It's not cool working with someone who hammers you every time on price, trying to get more for themselves and unwilling to give an inch. If you're too tough, it'll get talked about, and

(continued)

the net benefit won't help you in the long run. You've got to make sure you're negotiating with the right intention, and that your counteroffers are reasonable. A mentor once told me, 'A great deal is always when both parties feel like they've won a little and lost a little'.

Create urgency

Put urgency behind your negotiation by telling them there's an end date for when the deal must be done, or you'll walk away. Kick them into gear.

Hold your ground

If you're negotiating and it's not a good deal for you, hold your ground and be firm. Even say, 'this isn't sounding like a win–win for both of us, and I only do win–win deals'. If that doesn't bring them around, walk away and be glad you dodged a bullet.

Have confidence

Have the confidence to ask. And if you don't, fake it. Every time I fly and I'm not in business class or an exit row I go to the counter and say, 'Hey guys, I've had a long day, and I've got really long legs. Do you have any spare seats in the exit row? I could do with the extra leg room'.

'No worries, Mr Spencer, let me have a look.' More often than not I get the exit row. Not asking is the same as getting a 'no', so you may as well ask, and you might get a 'yes'!

Have fun

Negotiating doesn't have to be aggressive, it's not 'tough talk'—in fact, it's usually much more successful when you're nice. Be playful. Have fun. Don't take yourself too seriously!

Utilise the competitive advantage

There's a competitive advantage to getting people off guard by not looking like the smartest person in the room and letting them think they're the big shot. It's why I never wear suits (unless I'm doing a million-dollar deal or I'm at a funeral).

In November 2017, I had a meeting with one of Australia's largest listed companies; they own more than 10 of Australia's big household brands. They have a market capitalisation close to $70 billion! We met in a super high-end office, with fantastic facilities and views of Melbourne—it was stunning. They brought in their heads of IT, heads of legal, heads of finance and heads of commercial. Then there was me—a 27-year-old CEO—with my 35-year-old commercial director. It's always best to have the same number of people on your side as on theirs when negotiating, so we were at an immediate disadvantage. We hadn't expected them to bring in all of their top executives! It was an intimidating room, particularly if you think about how much all of their executives get paid—it was a lot of money being spent on one meeting.

They opened the meeting with politically correct corporate lingo, saying all the right long words and sounding impressive. They were discussing the ways the deal might

(continued)

MICK'S TIPS FOR BEING A GREAT NEGOTIATOR *(CONT'D)*

need to be structured, and it sounded way too complicated to me. They were all very smart individuals who were wanting to make this deal happen, but they were over-complicating it and playing the 'my laptop is bigger than yours' game. I looked like the little guy and I was okay with that. After listening carefully for 20 minutes, I piped up. 'Guys, let's just get this tactical, and on one page, with some end dates. Because if this deal is not done by [x date], I'll walk away.' Everyone shut up, stunned. 'Sorry to be blunt. I just don't want to waste your time, or mine. So let's all agree on some milestones.'

And we did. I utilised the competitive edge of being the little guy to my advantage.

Get a person from 'no' to 'maybe', and 'maybe' to 'yes'

How do you turn a 'no' into a 'yes'? First, be so damn passionate about making it happen that you will literally do anything to get a 'yes'. If you don't feel that way, is this something you really want to pursue? If you do feel that way, great!

Ask questions so you can understand what's holding the person back. Is it budget? Time? Personality? Great sales is about knowing the other person and getting inside their head—thinking how they're thinking. Learn what's stopping them from saying 'yes' so you can address those concerns.

Brett, a great employee of mine, came to me the other day because he was having some challenges closing a university he had already visited three times. I said, 'My first sale after delivering the 400 cycling jerseys took me 13 calls to close. On the twelfth call I was ready to give up, but it was that last one that made the difference'. It's all about persistence. Turn a 'no' into a 'maybe', and a 'maybe' into a 'yes'. How can you go the extra mile? How can you wow them? Be persistent. Be passionate. Get inside their head to understand their point of view.

There will be a lot of 'no's' when you're desperately seeking a single 'yes'. Sometimes you'll go home dejected. It sucks. I've heard far more 'no's' than 'yes's' on my journey. But guess what? It only takes a single 'yes' to turn things around, and you never know where that 'yes' will come from.

Believe the sale is true before it is

In my view, if you want something to happen, you must believe it ahead of it happening. It's not 'the secret'; it's making your mind believe something so that you approach it with total confidence and calm, already clear in your mind of the outcome. I have always focused on doing things like I can win, no matter what I'm doing—whether it's an investment deal, a sale, employing staff or completing a project. It's a must to believe in yourself and what you're doing before you do it. You won't win everything, nor should you—no-one deserves that—but with a total belief in yourself you'll start making great progress.

Rejection

This is a big one: it's painful and sucky. In life, we're faced with rejection all the time: relationship breakups, not getting the pay rise you expected, not getting that apartment you wanted to buy, not getting into the university course you so desperately wanted.

For me rejection started young. I was socially rejected because I was the odd one out—with my coke-bottle-thick glasses, being chubby and short—and it affected me big time. I was a target for bullying, which gave me a constant feeling of rejection. As an adult, I've experienced a lot of rejection too. I've walked in to pitch to prospective clients, excited about the great things we could do, to have them completely turn me down, not getting what I'm on about. I've had staff who I saw the best in—who I developed and mentored and gave my all to; or who I had sleep at my house to get us by when we had no money to pay for accommodation—reject me with their ungratefulness. It was painful and hard to realise that my baby had been broken by people who I thought were dependable and had the company's best interests at heart. I've walked in to many investor meetings and pitches after days of intense preparation, so passionate about what I'm building and the path I'm going to take the investors on, for them to say, after showing great interest, 'let's relook at it in 12 months'. That is code for a big fat 'we're not going to invest in you'. I've put in heaps of hours to submit tenders and then haven't been short-listed. Even more painful is when we've been short-listed, we've become super pumped, hoping to get first place, only to get second place—*just* missing out on the deal. Second place is first loser, and it doesn't feel good.

Getting rejected is a natural part of progress. To make things happen you need to put yourself out there, make big asks and accept that not everything will come back with a nice 'yes'. You may apply for jobs you won't get. You may ask for pay rises you won't get. You may work your guts out for three years on a start-up that collapses. The goal isn't to avoid rejection, it's to collect as much rejection as you can. To put yourself out there so much that you're getting rejected flat out. The higher the number of rejections you get, the higher the number of 'yes's' you'll get. Rejection is a learning curve that forces us to look at why we got a 'no', and what we can do differently next time to get a 'yes'.

A lot of the successful people I know are immune to rejection; they understand it's a natural part of progression, so they accept that they must face rejection head on. In fact, there's a popular TED talk, 'What I Learned From 100 Days of Rejection', that talks about how useful it can be to purposefully seek out rejection, every day, for something little—like asking to speak over a supermarket's intercom—so you can build your immunity to hearing 'no'.

As I'm becoming more immune to rejection, I'm becoming a stronger and more confident person. I get through rejection by remembering that it's all a part of the journey, and that no-one won the first time. Maybe I didn't win this time because of politics, or because I wasn't good enough. I get through it by looking at it rationally, and never letting it stop me. I don't let it get me down. Instead I analyse what we can learn from it—how we can do better next time—and I move on.

Fear and self-doubt

Fear and self-doubt will always be around; there's no magical way to remove them. It helps to remember that everyone experiences them, and the only way out is to push through. So many people are fearful they'll lose their job. I know musicians who are fearful they won't make it, and when they do make it they're fearful they'll lose it. I know millionaires who are fearful of losing their money and having to start again. I know billionaires who are fearful of things going horribly wrong and losing the majority of their wealth, along with their reputation. When I realised that some of the brightest sparks I know go through similar personal struggles, it helped me be less bothered by mine and face them head on.

But still, in the back of my mind there are those nagging questions that kindle my fears: How much money do we have? Can we pay our bills? Is that new customer going to sign? Is so-and-so going to do wrong by me? Am I staying healthy enough? Have I progressed far enough to meet my three-year goals? Can I really get there? Am I burning the candle at both ends? Am I disciplined? Are we training and developing the team enough? Do we have enough money to fuel growth? How is this contract going to go? Is this all real? Are we really going to get there or will I fall over? I have fears in my personal life as well. Am I being a great uncle to my nephews? Do I spend enough time with my family? Am I travelling too much and not spending enough time with my fiancée? Do I spend enough time with each close friend in my life? Fear and self-doubt can be all-consuming.

How to manage fear and self-doubt

I've come to peace with the fact that fear and self-doubt will always be there, so I manage them as best I can. When I feel fear or self-doubt rise up, the first thing I do is take away the intensity from the emotion. Becoming somewhat rational when I'm in an emotional state is something I'm constantly learning more about, and the more I do learn, the further I get. The fact is, when you're feeling doubt or fear you can choose to let it take you down, or to empower you. You can't be mellow with it; it's either up or down. When it kicks in I remind myself that it's just a part of the journey and I look at it with as little emotion as I can. 'Okay, it's happening. Can I deal with it or not?' I dig deep, knowing that it will go away if I just keep going.

In a practical sense, I get through the fear by hedging my risks so I'm managing what could go wrong, and I get through the doubt by having great people around me who I can openly talk to about it. This is why it's really crucial to have a great ecosystem of people to whom you can say, 'Mate, I may look like a superstar leading the charge, but I'm feeling rubbish'. My chairman is like a father figure in my business. I've got a great relationship with my father. I have the most beautiful fiancée, and I've got other people close to me who put things in perspective. When I'm concerned about doing a multimillion-dollar deal and a friend tells me about problems they're having with their children—maybe bullying at school—it snaps me out of it. It puts what I'm doing into perspective, and it all feels less terrifying.

Making sure I've had enough sleep always helps me, as well as keeping myself refreshed with habits and routines. I'm not a meditator in the sense of sitting still, but I leave things at home and go for a mountain bike ride. Moving my body breaks my emotional state, and there's nothing like riding in the mountains with good people, legs pumping, breathing in the fresh mountain air; the trees are just as they were yesterday and last year—no matter my ups and downs, they're a refreshing constant. This is how I keep method to the madness. You need to find the routine and habits that work for you.

TAKE A MOMENT

Half the time when you think you're feeling fear or doubt about something, it could actually be something unrelated. Look at the environmental factors affecting you. Are you tired, or overwhelmed? Are you hungry? When was the last time you were out in nature, or called a loved one? Maybe you're feeling lonely, or depleted, and once you reach out to connect to others, and have some quiet moments to connect with yourself, you'll feel a whole lot better.

What are you self doubts? Are you aware of them?

JOT DOWN YOUR THOUGHTS HERE

MICK'S TIPS FOR DEALING WITH FEAR AND SELF-DOUBT

Here are some useful questions that help me move through feelings of fear, self-doubt and overwhelm. Try asking yourself these when you need some reassurance.

- What is it that I'm fearful of?
- Am I being progressive in getting emotional about it?
- What does success look like from here?
- Who might be able to assist me with this issue?

The imposter syndrome

The imposter syndrome strikes almost every successful person. It's the experience of feeling that your accomplishments are somehow not real, and that you're a fraud who could be found out. I go through it a lot actually, thinking I'm a fraud and that somehow my achievements are fake, but it wasn't until I saw fellow Australian, legend and entrepreneur Mike Cannon-Brookes discuss the imposter syndrome in his TED talk that I put a name to the feeling I'd had so often.

Mike has a great story! He began his company Atlassian with his best buddy, Scott, after finishing uni, and it now has a revenue of over $600 million, a market valuation of $15 billion and employs thousands of staff! For 15 years he had this feeling every day that he didn't actually know what he was doing and that he would be found out—and he finally placed it as being imposter syndrome. It's really common.

When I was 20 I set the goal to have a $20-plus million business by the time I was 30. When I was 27, OTG was valued at over $20 million. I was three years early. It's crazy to think that in 2012 OTG was nothing but an idea! Is this all real? I remember later thinking, 'Wow, wouldn't it be great if one of the biggest companies in Australia wanted to work for us?' And then I reached the point where we started doing deals with that company and I thought, 'Imagine if I asked them for an investment?!' And then I got to the point of doing that, and they were keen as mustard. 'Holy shit', I thought. 'Is this real? Is someone going to tap me on the shoulder and say, "Just joking! Your time's up, mate!"'

The thing that helps me the most with the imposter syndrome is having mentors who have already reached my goals. That way, rather than feeling weird because it doesn't seem real, I have someone to validate my experience and say, 'Yes it is real, I've done the same thing too'. They help me settle into the reality more comfortably—it's important to have people around you who help make reality out of your dreams. Do you have these people? I've invested in a leadership team (my chairman and executives) who set the company's objectives with me, and they help make it all feel real when we achieve our goals.

It's also helpful to accept that feeling like an imposter happens, so don't let it get to you. As ambitious people, we often set the bar so high that when we get there we can't fathom that we've reached our goal. Take a moment to acknowledge what you've achieved—celebrate and ground yourself in the reality of your achievement. Go hang out with loved ones, feel the pride of making your goals happen. And then, set the next goal. My vision for 2022 is to take my company above $100 million. It's been a calendar reminder for a few years, every single day at 8.00 am (obsessed much?!). Moving on to the next goal keeps me active and engaged, and means there's not too much time to wallow in the feelings of being an imposter.

Give less fucks

At the end of the day, it's important to remember that life is way too important and short to give a shit about most things. In five years' time, will you really be worried and stressed about this? Keep your focus on the bigger picture, and give less fucks about everything else. Don't let things upset you that aren't worth your time, emotion or energy. Remind yourself that you'll die one day, so there really is no time to worry and stress about the majority of things you're worrying and stressing about. So, if in five years' time you won't care about something anymore, stop caring now.

ROUNDUP

- Being successful means facing some hard-hitting truths about life and facing your fears about whether you've got what it takes.
- There are six smarts you should focus on if you're looking for success: be informed, be selective, be open, be determined, be committed and never stop learning. And remember: we're all smart at what we're smart at.
- You'd be surprised what you can pull off if you fake it—so don't turn down amazing opportunities just because you're worried you might not be ready for them.
- Build your parachute: it's vital to have a network of people around you who believe in you and what you can achieve.
- Hard conversations are a part of life. Setting expectations early is the best way to make what would be a hard conversation easier.
- Selling is about asking questions to find out what problems people need solved, listening carefully to their answers and then finding a win–win.
- Make sure you give negotiations your full attention so you don't get fooled. Once the deal's done, there's no turning back.
- If you're persistent, there's a good chance you can turn a 'no' into a 'maybe', and a 'maybe' into a 'yes'.

- Get inside the other person's head to understand their point of view and then wow them with your passion.
- To make a sale, you have to believe in yourself and in what you're doing before you actually do it.
- Don't try to avoid rejection. It's a learning curve that forces you to think about why you got a 'no' and to turn it into a 'yes' next time around.
- Don't let fear or doubt get you down. Choose to be empowered instead by looking at things with as little emotion as possible.
- Ambitious people set the bar high, so sometimes when they reach their goals they feel like frauds—like their accomplishments can't possibly be real. That's the imposter syndrome kicking in. Don't dwell on the feeling: ground yourself in the reality of your achievement and set your next goal.
- Don't sweat the small stuff. Keep your focus on the bigger picture and don't let things upset you that aren't worth the time, emotion or energy.

YOU NEVER KNOW WHEN
SOMETHING CAN KNOCK YOU OVER

STAY
HUMBLE

KEEP WORKING

HARD AND
SMART

CHAPTER 8

GIVE LIFE YOUR ALL

My dad, Greg, said, 'I never pushed my kids into anything. You've got to be happy in what you do. When you get up in the morning and start the day, just remember that if you screw up this day you'll never get an opportunity to relive it. Every day matters. And Michael uses it in his tagline. That really tickles me pink'.

I'm the youngest of three children, which was great because I was, of course, spoiled and doted on, and I got to do a lot of things my two older siblings didn't (or so I'm still told!). We grew up in a small home in Canberra, Australia. My dad was a carpenter and businessman; my mother a nurse and then a midwife. With their mutual passions for building and decorating, we were always living in a house that was getting renovated around us.

We're an active family: the whole house was always awake and busy at 6 am. We had our own sets of chores to do, were always busy and my parents gave us an understanding of what it means to 'have the hustle'. Mum and Dad put us through school, fed us, clothed us and housed us, but if we wanted anything more we worked for it and bought it ourselves. We lived very simply and never believed in anything too extravagant. Mum and Dad taught us the simple principles for living a good life: work hard, be honest, never let fear stand in the way and always give 100 per cent in the work you do.

Dad got up early to go to work each morning, and would travel if there wasn't any work in Canberra. He always did what he needed to survive and prosper, but no matter how far he had to travel for jobs, he was always home for dinner. Even if he still had work to finish that night, he would come home first to have dinner with us before going back to the building site. He taught us to never give in to fear, and to take calculated risks. And we learned by example to do what we love and be grateful for the opportunities handed to us as well as those we had to fight for.

In the early days of OTG there were many dinner table conversations about the numbers in my business, with Dad ensuring that I knew what 'cash in, cash out, cash at bank' truly meant, as well as cost and risk analysis. I am *very* far from an accountant, but keeping those basic fundamentals intact assured me a good run. I was lucky to have had my brother and my father helping me from such a young age on these simple fundamentals.

Mum is the calming influence in the family; she brings everybody together when the shit hits the fan. She's been very successful in her own right—after becoming a nurse she rose through the ranks in the hospital she worked at, becoming the leader of the nursing unit. In her mid 30s she went into midwifery and, though she doesn't admit it, she's one of Australia's best midwives. She has helped to write a Midwifery curriculum for a university that offers a Bachelor Degree in Midwifery, the first of its kind in Australia. A passionate agent for change in her field, Mum has become the go-to person on the subject for the media, educators and innovators.

My dad comes from a family of five kids. He always wanted to be a carpenter because he was good with his hands and found joy in creating things, but his parents were conservative and had different ideas about what his career should be. Despite the opposition, Dad followed his heart and never looked back. Going against their wishes, he started an apprenticeship, which meant he had to move out of home. He couldn't afford rent so he lived out of his station wagon for the first year. At any point he could have gone back home saying, 'You know what, you're right. It's too hard out there. I'll follow the easy path', but Dad wasn't like that. He knew what he wanted, he knew where his passion lay and he was determined to get there even if it meant he was, literally, homeless.

My mum was born in a rural, country town to a Catholic family. Mum's dad was an extraordinary engineer, one of the first people involved in radio technology in Canberra. Mum and Dad met in their teens and were friends for years, both seeing other people, until they finally got together (their friends all saw it coming, but they took longer to cotton on).

Dad finished his apprenticeship and knew he didn't want to work for somebody else; he could do the work better and make more money doing it himself. He was 21 when he launched his commercial carpentry company, and Mum and Dad lived out in the suburbs in a tiny house for years. By the time I was born, Dad's business was growing, and it became the largest firm building commercial buildings in the region.

When I was 14, Dad had a big contract with a large listed company in the United States to build a massive data centre. Dad's business was pretty big at this point—he had over 40 staff, and they began construction for the data centre. Soon afterwards, the US company went into liquidation, owing Dad over $1 million for the work he had already completed. For months Dad went to countless creditor meetings to see how many cents on the dollar he could get, but ultimately he never saw a cent from them. The whole family's wealth was on the line; it was very real. Looking back it was good for us kids to go through the experience in that we all learned that this is what can happen. You never know when something can knock you over. Stay humble. Keep working hard and smart.

Though Dad didn't get paid, he still paid all of his contractors and staff for their work, which created a $1.5 million deficit for his company. His business was close to going broke. But Dad and his business partner were exceptionally hard workers—and smart. I remember them saying, 'We'll never let the company go broke'. Mum supported Dad totally. I remember conversations around the dinner table with her saying, 'If I need to work more shifts at work, I will'. It taught us kids the importance of rallying together to get through tough times.

Dad and his business partner pushed through the difficulties, grew the business and ultimately prospered. Dad's journey has inspired me greatly. He never built his business to become a millionaire. He built it to support the family. And that has stuck with all of us kids: the value of family. Dad taught us to never live beyond our means, and that we'd have to work hard for every dollar we earned. He also taught me that relationships get you through tough times. No-one speaks ill of my father, and it's because he's understood the value of relationships his whole life.

When my brother, Nathan, was 22 years old, he was working for Dad on a building site and he walked on a suspended ceiling that collapsed under his weight. He fell 14 metres into an auditorium, breaking both legs, both arms and the lower vertebrae of his spine. At that moment my dad walked onto the job site and saw his son in a pool of blood. He thought Nathan was dead. In fact, he is lucky to be alive. He was newly married at the time, young and fit—and then this accident happened. It was awful.

On top of the tough recovery my brother was going through, my dad was being sued by the insurance company for workplace negligence, even though it was in relation to his own son! They were working by the book—it's how insurance works—but it was a horrible time. Nathan was in hospital for three months and in a wheelchair for six months.

Twelve months after the accident, Nathan started to walk again! He was beginning to get back into life when his wife divorced him. Nathan turned to his hobby, cycling, and with persistence managed to teach his body how to cycle. He ended up being in the top three cross-country mountain bikers in Australia! It was incredible watching him push through and prove the doctors wrong. Today he's still very fit, and he's very successful. He's now a developer and builder, though he can't legally be on the tools himself. He's made his own fortune. He's still pushing through every day, and he motivates me and all those around him. Six years ago he married a beautiful woman, and they have two lovely babies with another one on the way! He's my best mate, and I look up to him every day. There's a lot of competition between us, but it's very healthy. As Winston Churchill famously said, 'Success is not final, failure is not fatal: it is the courage to continue that counts'.

My sister, Alicia, is also a total legend. She was OTG's third employee and helped the business enormously through an intense growth phase in 2013. I had been burned by a few people by this point, so it was amazing to have someone I could totally trust with the finances, with people and with HR. She came in when things were crazy, and she helped bind everything together and get people and processes working. She had had experience in business before, and was having kids at the time so the flexible hours worked well for her. She quickly became OTG's second-in-command and stayed with us until 2016. She did well because of OTG and also progressed her career and wealth. It's always tough working with family, but it was so great to see her prosper. She was a champion when I needed one.

My dad has the same heart condition as I do: atrial fibrillation (AF). Several years ago he underwent a medical procedure called catheter ablation that treats AF. This involves a tiny part of your heart being burned away, but in Dad's case too much was burned (which is exceptionally rare) and he lost a lot of blood. He died on the operating table, but they restarted his heart, which fortunately brought him back.

Our hearts sit in a sac, called the pericardium, and are surrounded by fluid. Because of the mishap on the operating table, Dad's blood now mixes with that fluid, which causes inflammation. It kills. This autoimmune disorder has totally changed his life. It's excruciatingly painful. It's awful seeing him in so much pain and being helpless to make it go away. A silver lining is that it has positively changed his perspective. He now goes away and does fun things he wouldn't have done before. It's made him relook at how he spends his days. Coming close to death makes you reconsider everything.

The doctors suggested that I have my heart burned too, but Dad's experience has put me off totally. As I have a big heart, the risks for me would be quite high. If there was a mishap, I could die or end up with a pacemaker. It would mean that I suddenly wouldn't be able to physically do a lot of what I do today. I prefer living life as I do now: I'm familiar with the conditions I've got, and I know what my limits are and how to handle my heart playing up.

There has been some concern recently that I may actually have ventricular tachycardia, (VT), as well as supraventricular tachycardia (SVT) and AF. My cardiologists haven't been able to determine, with certainty, that I don't. VT is fatal. It's very, very scary. They're still analysing me every six months, and they will for a few more years until my heart has finished growing, which for men is usually around 30. The other concern is that we don't know what long-term impacts the rapid beat of SVT has had on my heart. People don't normally have SVT or AF at a young age, so there isn't a case of a heart going through that strain from so early on. What will my heart be like at 60? At 70? Your heart is a skeletal muscle. What damage has the strain of all the episodes I've had at 240 beats per minute done? We don't know. That's why, for me, every moment counts.

Get shit done

My heart is a big reason why I live every day at 120 per cent. I love fast cars over golf. I love more rather than less. I love speed rather than going slowly.

A mentor once told me that the only currency worth treating as extremely valuable is time. As I said earlier, time competes with time.

TAKE A MOMENT

How do you manage your time? Do you actively monitor how you spend every hour—every 10 minutes—to make the most out of it?

JOT DOWN YOUR THOUGHTS HERE

Managing your time doesn't mean you have to always be working. As you know, I love time in nature, time with loved ones and time to unwind. But I'm always aware of what I'm doing with my time and I actively plan each day. Here are some planning tools you can use to do the same. These have be tried and tested by some of Australia's best executives.

The Daily Rocks planner

A few years ago, I was going through complete overwhelm in my business and personal life. Four of my five staff left, there was no certainty about the future of my business and my relationship broke down. I saw an NLP (neuro-linguistic programming) coach, and she taught me the value of the colours red, green and blue, by explaining to me what they mean. She also taught me the basic fundamentals of time management: lists, and putting everything on paper. There's a natural connection when putting pen to paper that helps the brain to connect to a task.

I live and die by this Red/Green/Blue planning document. It's such a strong habit that I feel lost without it. I call it my Daily Rocks. You can structure it to be for daily or weekly use, depending on how far you want to push your accountability. It's great for every application: whether you want to use it for work, for study or for planning your wedding. I have it completed by 7.30 am every day, no matter where I am or how tired or hungover I feel.

REDS

The things that you do not want to do, but you need to do. These are the tasks that are not always enjoyable, but need to happen.

They could be:

- replying to X person about Y problem
- submitting tax summary Z.

GREENS

The things that you want to do, but that can probably wait. These are the tasks that you enjoy doing, though they don't have any time pressure. It's important to consistently do a few of these things among the Reds and Blues.

They could be:

- creating X product sketch
- catching up with Y for coffee.

BLUES

These are the things that are all about growth, as an individual and in your cause/career/business, and they are the money-earning tasks.

They could be:

- closing X deal with Y
- learning A so you can accomplish B.

TAKE A MOMENT

Let's get your first day underway. By 7.30 am fill this in, and assess it through the day. The key is getting the important things done first; the rest will follow. Put a tick in the box if the task is completed, or put a cross if it isn't done.

REDS: WHAT MUST GET DONE, BUT YOU PROBABLY DON'T WANT TO DO

- ☐ ____________________
- ☐ ____________________
- ☐ ____________________
- ☐ ____________________

GREENS: WHAT YOU LOVE DOING, BUT CAN PROBABLY WAIT

- ☐ ____________________
- ☐ ____________________
- ☐ ____________________
- ☐ ____________________

BLUES: WHAT MAKES MONEY, AND IS GROWTH RELATED

- ☐ ____________________
- ☐ ____________________
- ☐ ____________________
- ☐ ____________________

The Daily Rocks planner helps you stay on top of all the tasks you need to be doing: those that are important that you don't enjoy; those that you do enjoy but aren't urgent; and those things that are directly related to your growth and income. It's important to have a mix of all three each day/week.

The Now/Future/How/What planner

An early mentor of mine, Brand Hoff, who sold his company for $200-plus million, taught me this method for keeping your plans lean and agile. You don't want your plans to be too in-depth and complex—things can change quickly and your plans need to be able to also.

This planner is useful for both your personal life and your cause/career/business. It asks four questions.

WHERE ARE YOU NOW?

List the measures that show you where you are right now. For example:

- What do you do for work, and how close is it to what you want to do?
- What is your personal salary?
- Where do you live?
- What size is your business?
- How many people do you work with?
- How much do you weigh?

WHERE DO YOU WANT TO BE?

Write down where you want to be in one year, in three years and in five years, listing the measures. For example:

- Where do you want to live, and in what kind of property?
- Who do you want to be around?
- What do you want to be earning?
- What goal/s do you want to have completed?

HOW DO YOU GET THERE?

What must you do to achieve where you want to be? For example:

- What tools do you need to get there?
- What people do you need to recruit to achieve the dream?
- What are the steps you need to take?

WHAT DO YOU NEED?

No-one can do it all on their own. What do you need to get to where you want to be? For example:

- How much time do you need?
- How much money do you need?
- What will the money be used for? How and when?

TAKE A MOMENT

What plans do you need to keep lean and agile? Add your own answers below.

WHERE ARE YOU NOW?

WHERE DO YOU WANT TO BE?

HOW DO YOU GET THERE?

WHAT DO YOU NEED?

The outsourcing guide

It often fascinates me that so many people will knowingly keep working hard at their weakness, thinking it will help in the long run. Focus on what you're great at, putting all your energy there. Collectively, as a team, we all do much greater work when each individual spends their effort doing what comes naturally to them. Now, if there are skills in your role that it would be useful to brush up on, do that. If you're terrible at spreadsheets but you're forcing yourself to do them, rather than getting out there and networking when that's your strength, stop. Pay someone or negotiate with someone to do the spreadsheets, and in return you can do what they're not great at (I talk more about this in the section 'Friend currency' in chapter 9). Not only is it better for productivity, it's better for work enjoyment. We often have more passion behind what comes naturally than what we're weak at.

I quickly learned to be happy with the truth: that I'm hopeless at some things. There was no point in fighting the fact that I wasn't going to learn like others in school, so why maintain that level of work if I was never going to be good at it? It didn't make sense. Instead, I applied myself to my young entrepreneurial schemes, to work and through that made money while learning what I really needed to know to run OTG successfully.

One of my mentors told me to deeply and specifically uncover what I'm great at, and what I'm not great at, and then to fill in people and processes where I'm weak. That way I could focus on my great strengths in business to propel my vision forward. I took this advice on board and became clear on what specific things I would do, and worked out from there what I would outsource.

In today's world, where we have access to many people who can assist us to achieve our goals and dreams, it's so worth outsourcing. There are amazing companies that connect emerging parts of the world with established economies to provide employment in struggling economies, and to offer more affordable workers to those living in stronger economies. At any time, OTG engages with more than 10 outsourcing freelancers who we've found on platforms such as freelancer.com, odesk.com, upwork, Zirtual ... and there are many more.

Take advantage of the talent around you, locally and globally. Look at how you spend your time each day, the return on investment (ROI) it's giving you, and where you could create efficiencies. Look at the tasks you're doing yourself, and the tasks you're paying a premium for, and research if there's someone overseas you can pay to do it more cheaply. Free up your schedule so you have more time to work on a project or take your career to the next level.

Outsourcing is not the way of the future: it's the way of today. As I've said, time competes with time, and you want to make sure you're getting an ROI for how you're spending your time. I have someone who does my ironing, my cleaning and my cooking because 1) I can now afford it, 2) I travel a lot with work and much prefer to spend the time I have at home with my fiancée and 3) when I calculated the money I spend on groceries and the time it takes to cook (when I could be working or resting for the next big day of work), the price was close. Having a cook come in was a no-brainer. Use outsourcing for life admin so you can spend that time more wisely yourself. Invest in your time.

Some typical tasks you can outsource are:

- calendar assistance and scheduling
- researching bars, sights or restaurants and making reservations

- booking holidays
- data entry
- financial modelling
- graphic design
- marketing tasks
- development of architectural plans
- writing and editing
- website development
- social media planning.

Some around-the-house jobs you can outsource are:

- cleaning
- clothes washing
- ironing
- cooking
- mowing
- gardening
- handyman jobs.

HOW TO MANAGE FREELANCERS

It's important to lay the expectations early on, and to keep people accountable to deadlines so they know to deliver on time—always.

Here's a role description template (overleaf) you can use when looking for a freelancer.

Task name: ______________________________

Project deliverables:

1) ______________________________
2) ______________________________
3) ______________________________
4) ______________________________

Due date: __/___/______

Reporting structure:

- Introductory session: 30 minutes via Skype
- Meet weekly for 15 minutes on X day
- Send email correspondence daily for questions by X time
- Have both parties sign a working arrangement

If you don't have a working arrangement handy, or have never used one before, search online to find one that will fit your needs.

Get and stay connected

Today it is very easy to be connected to the people you're working with, no matter their location.

Here are the tools I use to constantly connect with people worldwide:

APP	TOP FEATURES
Skype/Skype for Business	Plan online meetings in advance and schedule them via Outlook Up to 250 people can join the meeting View up to 6 people on your screen in 1080p resolution Share desktop screens Free video/audio calls Instant messaging
WhatsApp	Available on phone and desktop Free video calls Record messages as opposed to typing them Share documents up to 100MB Group chat feature Instant messaging
WeChat	Extremely popular in China; perfect for connecting with other people overseas Translate messages from any language into English Free video calls to anyone else in the world Available on phone and desktop Group chat feature Instant messaging

(continued)

APP	TOP FEATURES
Viber	Free HD video calls Group chat feature App syncs with other devices Instant messaging Charged international calls Share files up to 200MB
Zoom	HD video cloud conferencing Group instant messaging Document sharing and screen sharing Basic plan 100% free

ROUNDUP

- When you get up in the morning and start the day, always remind yourself that if you screw up this day you'll never get an opportunity to relive it.
- You'll encounter tough times—possibly financially or even health-wise. If your livelihood is on the line through no fault of your own, stay humble and work hard and smart.
- Value relationships—especially those with your family.
- You don't have to come close to dying to reconsider life and relook at how you spend your days, as I did. So try to live your life fully now.
- Plan your time on a weekly or daily basis using the planners in this chapter.
- Take advantage of the talent around you to make your life more efficient—there are so many tasks that can be outsourced, freeing up your time to do the things you're best at.
- Remember to stay connected to the people you are working with, no matter where they're located.

THERE'S POWER
IN HAVING LESS
AND EVEN MORE
IMPORTANTLY
IN BEING
HAPPY
WITH LESS

CHAPTER 9
THE POWER OF LESS

Most people are caught up in *more*. They want more, buy more, want to have more and they lose sight of *the power of less*. If you give a monkey a banana when it's hungry, it's ecstatic and gobbles it up. If you give it another banana it's ecstatic again, even though it's already full from the first. If you then take that second banana away from it, it will be furious. It doesn't need that second banana now, but it wants it. Humans are much the same: we want many, many things we don't need.

There's a great book by William B Irvine called *A Guide to the Good Life: The Ancient Art of Stoic Joy*, which teaches the wisdom of the ancient Greek philosophy of Stoicism. I love it because it teaches many great principles and daily practices. One that stands out is the power of 'negative thinking', a technique practised in meditation where you think constantly about losing valuable possessions, and of loved ones dying. The ancient Greeks lived in abundance and easily got lost in the constant desire for more, so they practised the idea of losing everything to keep them grateful and humble. It worked incredibly well.

In his book, Irvine writes, 'The easiest way for us to gain happiness is to learn to want the things we already have'. There's power in having less and, even more importantly, in being happy with less. I live a minimalist life because I'm happier with less—it keeps my mind clear. I have a simple wardrobe, and I don't spend a lot of money on clothes. I wear recycled fabrics and recycle my wardrobe regularly (at OTG we run charity programs where we give sports gear to communities in need in Western Australia). My home is minimalist and uncluttered. It's about going to bed feeling clear, and waking up feeling clear. I ensure we have a clean workplace at OTG, I don't overpack when I travel and I don't buy more groceries than I need. I always make my bed the moment I get up, and I don't leave things lying around. If we're too busy to clean the apartment, we get our cleaner in because the cost is totally worth it for clearer headspace.

The challenge people have is that when they earn more, they spend more because their focus is on having *more* rather than appreciating what they *already have*. Advertising doesn't help, convincing people to hand over their hard-earned cash for things they don't need. Phones are crowded with apps, inboxes are full of clutter and rubbish, cupboards are overflowing, houses are cluttered and garages are a mess!

The goal is to be happy with a basic, simple, cheap and uncluttered life. I was living off roughly $30 000 a year for the first two years of OTG. In fact, my tax return in my first year of business shows my income was $25 400, and my tax return for my second year was $32 000. And I was happy! I loved what I was doing; I was working to my purpose. I was building my vision. Life was good. I didn't need a lot.

TAKE A MOMENT

How does living a cluttered life affect you? Do you focus on wanting more? If so, how could you instead appreciate what you already have? Is it time to do a massive de-clutter of your life?

What can you do to remove the need for 'more'?

JOT DOWN YOUR THOUGHTS HERE

Analyse what you need to survive, fundamentally, and then throw in a few nice-to-haves. Then get rid of the rest, donating it all to charities. Being minimalist doesn't mean you don't have anything nice. It means being conscious about what you have, what you actually need and what you really love, and getting rid of the rest. I own two mountain bikes and a road bike because I love cycling, and I have a great surfboard because I love surfing. They're my nice-to-haves, and I only purchased them when I could easily afford them. Don't buy things you won't use, and get great usage out of the things you do buy. Remember: most of the things that are important in life don't cost much money.

Sacrifice

For the first four years of OTG I sacrificed earning decent money. I sacrificed holidays, overseas travel, buying property, buying a car, buying clothes, going out for drinks or dinner with mates, going to music festivals and relaxing on weekends. I was focused on what I was building because my purpose was bigger than myself. I saw my business as being very important for people, providing work for Australian staff and for contractors and factory workers overseas, making customers really happy and changing an industry. We invested all our earnings back into OTG. Everything I have earned since has been icing on the cake. I appreciate it, and I don't take it for granted.

TAKE A MOMENT

What can you sacrifice? What are you spending money and time on that isn't worth it?

What can you live without?

JOT DOWN YOUR THOUGHTS HERE

Money money money

In his book *The Richest Man in Babylon,* George S Clason says, 'Plan your budget in that way, that money will be enough for necessary needs, pleasure and worthy of desire, but the costs do not exceed nine-tenths of the income'. People often meet their income with their expenses, but treating money that way keeps people struggling. Clason's book is one of the best books on money management. I highly recommend reading it if what I share in this section is new to you.

Money intrinsically has no value. It's what you do with that money that has value. You can't eat money, or drive money, but you can use money to buy food, and to buy a car or to pay for public transport. To manage money effectively, keep it simple. One rule that's good to follow is to save 10 per cent of your income every pay cheque—have 10 per cent automatically transferred into a savings account. Another good rule is to measure your debit and credit every day. Keep track of all money coming in, and all money going out. Know exactly what you're doing with your money, and how your bank account is looking—every day. Make sure you're spending on the right things.

It's important to map this out in alignment with your career goals. For example, let's say that in one year you want to get a $10 000 pay rise. How do you do that? For a $10 000 pay rise you may need to be more educated in X topic, so that you can argue you're providing a stronger ROI to your boss. Or, show your boss that with a 10 per cent pay rise you're going to increase your productivity and effort by 30 per cent, and measure it to show them how you'll do it. What's important is to show your boss how the pay rise will deliver results for the company. Another way to negotiate a pay rise is to look for alternative roles, or employers.

TAKE A MOMENT

Where are you financially right now? Calculate your cash, your assets, your good debt (which is your assets, e.g. a house) and your bad debt (e.g. credit card debt, a loan for a car).

Now, where do you want to be financially in six months? In one year? In five years?

What do you need to do to get there?

JOT DOWN YOUR THOUGHTS HERE

Let's say that in one year you want to have $5000 to invest in the stock market. How do you get there? You need to put $417 a month into savings, which means you need to save $96 a week, and to do that you need to sacrifice something else. What do you really need each week, and what can you sacrifice so you can save $96? Keep in mind that it's often the little, *consistent* sacrifices that add up to the big savings.

There are some great apps that help you budget your money better and save more. My personal favourites for budgeting are My Budget and Money Brilliant. The best app I've found for tracking expenses is Wally, and the best app for painless saving is Acorns (now named Raiz). Check them out!

	My Budget	*Wally*	*Raiz (formerly Acorns)*	*Money Brilliant*
Free	✓	✓	×	✓
Budgeting	✓	✓	×	✓
Track payments	✓	✓	✓	✓
Net worth tracking	×	×	✓	✓
Goal tracking	✓	✓	×	✓
Android	✓	✓	✓	✓
iPhone	✓	✓	✓	✓
iPad	×	×	×	✓
Desktop	×	×	×	✓

Keep your financial plan simple, and keep it in sight. I have a 10-year business plan on one page that sits right next to my desk, and as the background on my iPhone and my iPad. I see it every day. I also have a calendar request at 8 am every day reminding me of the date I'm going to have a billion-dollar company.

Every six months, or earlier, *revisit your budget*. Have it in front of you. Any money that you can save can be invested. Investments will build long-term cash flow through dividends, and will build equity. Today, if I have spare money I will either invest it and earn something out of it, or I'll give it away in a way that teaches and empowers someone. For example, if I give $1000 to people I know in Fiji or Western Australia, it makes a big difference to their lives. Make sure you get an ROI out of everything you do, whether it's a financial ROI, or helping someone. At OTG we have supported over 15 charities, and we give social grants every quarter to help individuals or communities who are raising money for a cause, or who need funding to get a local sports team off the ground so there is somewhere positive for youth to go.

There's nothing wrong with being a tight-arse

Being a tight-arse is rare nowadays, but it's an essential financial skill to learn. A 2018 financial planner would call the younger generation the 'smashed avo on toast' group. We live in a world based so much more on convenience now than net equity. To increase your savings you need to 1) look at how you can increase your income and 2) look at how you can decrease your spending. Being a tight-arse means you're spending less and saving more — it's fantastic! It's a method you shouldn't stop, and the earlier you get into it, the better you'll be long term. The journey of an entrepreneur can be up and down, and overnight you can become a millionaire, but it's so important to stay consistent as we've seen too many highs and lows with successful founders and executives.

For OTG to be able to exhibit at expos in the first few years, we had to maximise our cash to afford the booth, so I slept in my car before the expo, never bought a drink at the evening events and would run to a local food court to find a cheap meal rather than spend $20 on lunch at the expo. It was *so* worth it.

To be a tight-arse you need to first get in touch with your current spending habits. In a note on your phone, or using one of the apps I suggest earlier, write down every time you spend $1 or more, for a month. Every single time. Yes, it'll take discipline. Do you want to live an extraordinary life? Because it takes work! At the end of each week, review your spending to see where your money is going. Then imagine you suddenly had half the income you have today—how would you make it work? Where can you sacrifice? Where can you be smart about saving a few dollars? If you're about to go out with friends, ask them how much what you're doing will cost, and explain that you won't spend any more than X. Make it clear, and put it back on the other person.

When was the last time you practised the art of being a tight-arse?

Friend currency

Another great way to be smart with your spending is to find people who can help you for free to do things that you would normally have to pay for. I call it 'friend currency'. As I've said, it's really worthwhile making the effort to meet many people in a broad range of fields, and to see who you genuinely click with and become friends with. You can then find a win–win situation where you can help them for free with something they need, and they can help you, removing the need for a financial transaction. Everyone wins.

For example, you may have a good friend who is a tradie and who agrees to do a small renovation for you where you only pay for materials, and because you're great at finance, in return you help them do a proper budget for their business and manage their cash flow better, easing their financial stress. That way they're getting value in their business, and you're getting equity in your home. It's a great contra for both parties.

Debt: the good and the bad

There are two kinds of debt: good debt and bad debt. Many Millennials are far too comfortable with the idea of being in debt, making building wealth for themselves so much harder. If you want to do well financially don't ever get into debt for depreciating assets or experiences. Only ever buy clothes, furniture, cars, holidays, tickets to music festivals and so on when you have the money available, *and when after the purchase you can still meet your saving targets.*

In general, there are two times when going into debt is a good idea: when you're building a business, and when you're buying a property. By borrowing more than you have you're leveraging yourself for growth, meaning you're borrowing money to buy the potential of earning more than you've borrowed (either through your business doing well, or through capital growth/rental returns on a property). How much is smart to borrow depends on your personal situation, and it's best to get financial advice from experts and mentors who have successfully done what you want to do.

What is good debt?

Good debt is when you use money to make money. As author Sol Luckman said: 'It takes money to make money'. You can use good debt to generate an income and to increase your net worth. Let's look at some examples of good debt.

BORROWING FOR SHARES IN YOUR OWN BUSINESS (OWNING A SMALL/GROWTH BUSINESS)

The best way to earn money without having to answer to a boss is to start your own business. An added benefit is that depending on how hard you're willing to work you can earn as much as you want. And if you're successful, you may be able to sell your business for a tidy profit down the track.

In the early stages, you have two choices: debt to the bank or debt to yourself. (Later on there is a third choice: debt to shareholders). The more you can be in debt to yourself, the better. Many people mistakenly think they need to have a lot of capital to get their business off the ground, but they forget that 'capital' is another word for 'debt'. Launching your business with a huge amount of debt is not a good strategy. Instead, look at what you can do with what you personally have, so you're only in debt to yourself. How far could you take the company on your own? It's much better doing more with less, and being really smart about your business spending.

Borrowing, and therefore using other people's money (OPM) to grow your business, is a smart decision when you have the right execution behind it, which takes learning and experience, and usually works out best when your business is somewhat established. Today I can make myself and my shareholders extremely wealthy using other people's money because I've learned how. Four years ago I had no idea how to do that. I'm so glad I took the journey on my own, being indebted to myself first, before using OPM. Now I am a far more compelling case to wealthy people because I got myself so far. They can see I know what I'm doing. Use OPM when you know how to. It's not a bad thing making other people wealthy, but be aware that it will come with pressure.

BORROWING TO BUY PROPERTY

There are several ways of making money through real estate. One way is to buy a house, live in it for a few years while adding value through renovations, and then sell it for a profit. You could also generate an income from the property by either taking in a boarder or renting out the house and living somewhere else. It's a great way to have a cash flow for future projects while building your equity base.

The most common way to use OPM is when buying property. Buying with a 10 per cent or 20 per cent deposit, and borrowing the rest, leverages the small amount of wealth you have today for potential capital growth over the next number of years. Though property is usually seen as an appreciating asset, it's important to be very careful what property you buy—a lot of people have been burned, believing that property prices would go up without realising there was an oversupply of properties in that area. They then find they have to sell their property five years later for the same amount they bought it for, or less. They not only lost money spent on buying, maintenance and selling costs, they also lost what that money could have earned them over those five years.

The other issue with property is that people borrow the maximum amount the bank will give them to buy the most expensive house 'they can afford'. It can be a disaster waiting to happen. What if you're retrenched and take three months to find another job? What if interest rates go up and your monthly mortgage repayments therefore increase? Suddenly your mortgage, which was already spreading you thin, tips you over the edge and you can't afford the monthly repayments. It becomes awful and stressful; you may end up being forced to sell; and it's totally unnecessary. You want to buy a property comfortably, with savings on the side after the purchase.

Before you buy a property, research whether you can utilise government grants or stamp duty concessions—for example, the First Home Owner Grant. Then, it's a race to see if you can pay it off. A tip from a millionaire friend of mine was 'never have debt on a non-deductible asset' (that is, your place of residence).

What is bad debt?

While even 'good debt' can turn bad if the business or property doesn't grow as planned, bad debt is anything you buy that won't go up in value or generate an income, so you shouldn't go into debt to buy it. Bad debt includes items such as:

- *cars*. Cars, especially new ones, are expensive, so don't add to the cost by borrowing money to buy a car. Avoid bad debt by buying a cheap, reliable, second-hand car that you can pay for in full on the day of purchase.
- *credit cards*. These are one of the worst types of bad debt because of their extremely high interest rates. Interest rates charged are almost always *way* higher than the rates on consumer loans. It's a good idea to avoid credit card debt, no matter what.

- *unnecessary consumables*. These include clothes, and other goods and services. I'm not saying you can never buy yourself a new piece of clothing, go out for a meal or go on a holiday, but you never want to go into debt for nonessential purchases. If you're ever tempted to buy a consumable or experience using a credit card, make sure you can pay it off within the interest-free period.

Investing

There are many options to choose from if you're looking to invest, such as stocks, bonds, commodities, futures and metals, and alternative investments. In general, short-term investing is used for generating an income, and long-term investing is for generating wealth. You can also invest in start-ups, though these are high risk, and it's best you have a lot of experience in business so you can make a good judgement of which start-ups might go big. If a start-up you invest in does go big, the reward is huge—you could retire off it! I've had investors become millionaires out of investing in me, and I've seen them invest in other now-successful companies that they have retired off. To invest in startups you need to be able to tolerate risk, and be able to stomach losing your money on a rough average of 9/10, because it might only be only 1/10 that pays off.

Investing often comes down to time: the more time you have your money invested for, the bigger your returns. Every six months that go by without investing is money you're throwing away. Be a tight-arse so you can save money to start investing! Maybe don't spend that $6000 on a second trip to Europe, and instead invest in your future. There are many Millennials who have spent so much money on travel in their 20s that they're crying poor as they approach 30. Yes, those adventures were fun and worth it, but you've also just thrown away 10 years of opportunity where your money could have been working for you, earning you more money.

The Australian Dream used to be to go to university, get a decent job, buy your own home, pay off the mortgage slowly, and then retire off the growth of the family home and your pension. But in many ways this dream has changed because 1) property is not the only effective way to grow future net worth, and 2) the pension is no longer enough to live off today, so by the time we Millennials retire, I can guarantee it won't be enough, particularly when you look at the population replacement statistics for Australia.

MICK'S TIPS FOR INVESTING

The most important thing for you to start doing this week is to invest in learning how to invest. Maybe you'll decide to buy a house, and five years later buy a second, and maybe another five years later buy a third. Or maybe you'll study investing in the stock market or index funds, or currencies, or angel investing in companies—and start doing that in a year with the money you save over the next 12 months. Whichever of the many strategies you choose, get started *now.*

Where are you now? Where do you want to be? How do you get there ... and what do you need?

One of the things I've learnt in building wealth in my business and personal life is identifying fundamentally where you are NOW. No bullshit. No glossy crap. Just identify exactly where you stand. Once you can do that, you've made the massive steps towards where you can or want to go.

Then it's about setting where you want to be, and by when. What I've found really important is putting dates to things. Often my staff will laugh at my calendar notifications; I actually make sure my key goals or targets have a reminder and due date ... otherwise, what's the point?

Using the guide that follows—for me it started on the back of a paper towel with the help of a business mentor, who founded a now $5 billion business called The North Face—I was shown that it's important to identify where the startup WAS. Where we wanted to BE. What we thought we needed to DO and HOW, and WHAT was required. This was when I first decided to sky-rocket the business and raise capital.

Now I use this chart to simplify business plans and goal lists, and even take it to my team for personal development. So, see my example on the following pages, and why don't you have a go yourself?

You can also download the chart from onthegosports.com .au/book

1. WHERE ARE YOU NOW?

- Savings (daily and storm)
- Investments in shares
- Property assets
- Assets and liabilities
- Assets – liabilities (net worth)
- Projects (what do you have 'happening')

____

____

2. WHERE DO YOU WANT TO BE?

3–6 months	*12–24 months*	*5 years*
(achievable, short-term, measurable)	*(once routine is created and you're measuring what is working, you will see results in this period)*	*(this is about being a little BHAG [Big Hairy Audacious Goal]; know that if you think big and act small you can reach it)*
Savings to $5K	Savings to $15K	Savings to $200K
Stocks valued at $10K	Stocks valued at $25K	Stocks valued at $150K
Net worth to be $50K	Net worth to be $100K	Net worth to be $500K
Spending less than X on Y		Pay off X mortgage

____

____

____

3. HOW DO YOU GET THERE?

- Measure my results weekly/monthly
- Set up a savings plan with goals
- Spend more time with like-minded people

4. WHAT DO YOU NEED TO DO?

- Move money from X to Y
- Sell X property before Y
- Set up high-interest-earning account X
- Schedule 1 hour per week for planning
- Book in for a learn to stock trade class by X date
- Buy 2 fewer coffees per week
- Set up an account with Raiz
- Sign up to Money Brilliant and plug all accounts together

ROUNDUP

- Most people are so caught up in wanting more of everything that they lose sight of *the power of less.* We all want many things that we don't need—learn the difference between a *want* and a *need.*
- The goal is to be happy with a basic, simple, cheap and uncluttered life. So analyse what you need to survive, fundamentally, and then throw in a few nice-to-haves (if you can afford them without going into debt).
- Learn to sacrifice by focusing on your purpose instead of spending money on unnecessary things such as holidays and cars—it's often the little, *consistent* sacrifices that add up to the big savings.
- Remember that money intrinsically has no value. It's what you do with money that has value. It's simple really: spend less, save more!
- To manage money effectively, automatically transfer 10 per cent of your income to a savings account, and keep track of your debit and credit every day.
- Keep your financial plan simple, and keep it in sight. Then, every six months or so, revisit your budget.
- Use friend currency to gets things done at no cost: you provide someone with something you're good at and in return they do the same—no money exchanged.

- Good debt is when you use money to make money—use good debt to generate an income and to increase your net worth.
- Bad debt is anything you buy that won't go up in value or generate an income, so you shouldn't go into debt to buy it.
- Don't use other people's money (OPM) to make money unless you know how to do it.
- In general, short-term investing is used for generating an income, and long-term investing is for generating wealth.

YOU NEED TO TRULY KNOW WHERE YOU WANT TO BE IN YOUR FUTURE, AND THEN

SURROUND YOURSELF

WITH THE TYPE OF PEOPLE WHO HAVE

BEEN THERE

OR ARE ON A SIMILAR PATH

CHAPTER 10

SHOOT FOR THE STARS, GET MENTORED AND MAKE IT HAPPEN

I'm a big believer in doing an excellent job in whatever you do. And if you see something being done in a terrible way, fixing it. Through delivering my first big order of 400 cycling jerseys I learned how the custom apparel industry would normally work. Most of OTG's big competitors have teams of 20, 50 and even up to 100 people to handle every step of the process: sales, design, development of the product, quality control, production management, tracking of where the order is up to, quality control before dispatch and delivery.

It would happen like this. A salesperson would meet with a client who wanted a custom-designed product to find out what they were after. The salesperson would talk to the graphic designer, who would develop a mood board of designs. The salesperson would take this mood board back to the customer and try to sell it. If they closed the deal, the graphic designer would talk to preproduction to get all the files ready for the factory. Then they would send the files to the factory, and pay the factory. The factory would likely have a lot of questions about the details of the items, and they would go back and forth until it was all ironed out. At this point the factory would manufacture the garments, quality control would check them, and then the order would be dispatched. The whole process usually took three months. Alternatively, a customer could drive to a store and choose from a limited number of plain-coloured shirts that were on the shelf, and from there figure out themselves how to get the shirts printed.

I remember thinking, 'Wow, this is a painfully long process for customers, and it's painfully complicated for the companies. Why? Let's make it simple'. I wanted to make it possible for someone sitting in a café, on their iPad, to design their own custom apparel then and there, with a wide range of choices for every part of the design. I wanted them to be able to click 'Order' and receive their garments in only a few weeks, rather than three months. And so I turned my mind to how I could improve the whole process. No-one in the industry had built a full, end-to-end system, but I was determined to figure it out.

I started with cycling garments first, for which we created the software automation for the cycling jerseys and bottoms. Then we built the cycling wind vest, and the cycling jacket. Then the long bottoms. Then someone asked if we could do basketball uniforms. We said 'yes', and built the files and automation for those uniforms. We took pre-ready files from the factory, learned where the gaps were for the basketball apparel, fixed the files, and with them made basketball jerseys followed by basketball shorts. Now we had another category! Then we built a category for soccer, and rugby, and volleyball, and netball, and today we have 20 different categories and over 1 million options.

We've achieved this by taking the effort we'd put into one product, prepopulating it, and utilising it again and again and again for other products. And while building these out, we were constantly iterating the serviceability. It wasn't all online and easy to begin with. We bootstrapped the business and slowly developed the technology, the software and our website. But from the beginning it was our service that was really different. Even when we didn't have the fully transactional website where people could design their products themselves, I made sure we had our offshore design teams sign a service level agreement to have a maximum turnaround time of 24 hours, whereas other companies were still taking weeks.

The road to the dream

After dropping out of uni to work on OTG full time, I learned everything I needed to run a business. I set up the accounting software, I did all my own bookkeeping, and I was selling and selling and selling like mad. Six months in, I got to the stage where I needed someone to help me with the order processing and other bits and pieces, so I brought in an intern. He loved the business, and once he'd finished the internship I was able to afford keeping him on as a staff member, which he was thrilled about. After another six months we were able to move out of my dad's wood-turning shed-cum-office, and into my mate Stuart Cook's office, where we rented a desk. Stuart was running what is now Australia's biggest Mexican franchise, Zambrero. Remember: you become who you mix with! In OTG's first year we did $100 000 in sales, and we were able to rent another desk at Stuart's office. In the second year we doubled, and in the third year, despite major setbacks, we doubled again.

Today we essentially operate at the intersection of the customer and the manufacturer: our business is a technology conduit for the factory and the customer to connect. Our customers choose the specific custom design they want themselves, click 'Order', and the factory instantly starts manufacturing their apparel. We've achieved this by investing in our software and ecosystem to make it possible for production files to be prepopulated. This means that the moment customers choose their custom design and click 'Order', it automatically prepopulates all of the production files ready for the factory to make that item on the same day. For example, we have a polo shirt with 20 available designs, and within each design option there are six panel and colour changes, with 50 colour options. So that polo shirt may have about 6000 options.

We got to this point with our ethos of continually iterating and improving our products, service and software. We've created efficiencies not only for our customers, but for our factories too. Our factories love us. There have been challenges because OTG has grown so quickly—there are always growing pains—but I'm proud of what we've done, and I'm excited about where we're going. Some companies have 400 staff doing what we're doing with 35.

Our team is like a family, and just because I'm the CEO doesn't mean I'm above anyone. I'm a team player—we all work together. It's essential to have that support for each other professionally and personally because you go through so much pain together. In a fast-growing company your position changes in six months and the company (now) doubles or triples in size in a year. When that kind of extreme growth happens, everything busts and breaks. I've consciously made sure I've built an environment where it's a 'one team one dream' ethos, and where we all support each other, and my executives have been critical to this. We have regular team meetings called Pow-Wow every week at 9 am on a Monday, which everyone attends—no matter what. And we have team outings every quarter to celebrate our success or failure from the previous three months.

Our company culture has to come from the top—me—and I'm inspired by how creating a supportive culture has transformed employees' lives. In fact, OTG's chief commercial officer, Michael, always says, 'You don't work at OTG, you live it. We're like a family'. People spend a large chunk of their life working, and knowing that I can provide them with work that's challenging and engaging, in a supportive environment, is awesome. I'm passionate about creating a hub where people's ideas and minds can flourish, and they can do anything they want to set their mind to.

Be transparent

I'm a transparent leader. I try to be vulnerable and real, and I believe it's so important to lead this way. It's part of what builds the trust and is why my team gives their all to accomplish miracles together.

I'm also transparent with our 'No Dickhead Policy' (NDP). I have a philosophy that life is too short and there's no point working with people who are dickheads. The other way of putting it, which I'm open and clear about, is 'Fit in or Fuck off!' (FIFO). It's important to be upfront with people, and to be able to have those hard conversations. In your career, you're going to come across people who are dickheads. It's best if you can avoid having to work with them, but sometimes that will be out of your control. What is in your control is whether you let them affect you, and what you say to them. I might say, 'Look, it seems as though you might have a problem with me. The fact is, we've got to work together. Are you okay? Is everything good with you? Because I'm feeling a bit of tension here, and I'd prefer if we could get on with it'. They might reply, 'Oh no, no, no, there's nothing. Sorry. I've been caught up with X and Y'. Or they might say, 'Yeah, there is something', to which I respond, 'Cool, let's open up about it. We've got to work together, so let's go for a five-minute walk. I'll drop everything I've got on because this is important'. Baggage is death! Have the conversations you need to have, clear the air and move on.

Get mentored

Mentors will massively accelerate your growth. Being mentored by someone who has already been where you want to go—who has achieved what you want to achieve—will propel you forward in whatever you do. Looking for a mentor to help you with your career, your business, your hobby, your relationships, and so on, will be one of the best things you do. There is nothing quite as awesome as learning from other people's mistakes and successes. How did they climb that corporate ladder? How did they pull off that deal? How did they handle those tricky conversations with stakeholders? How did they negotiate a pay rise? How do they network? How do they manage their habits to get the most out of each day? Having a mentor puts another voice in your head when it comes to making decisions. What would X do? Would they go this route, or maybe try this?

You've probably heard the phrase 'plug and play' associated with computers. You just plug in the hardware (keyboard, mouse or whatever it is) and the operating system recognises it automatically, installing the appropriate software, and it's ready to use almost instantly. I use the same phrase for mentors. A 'plug and play' mentor plugs into your life at the right time and is ready to help with the set of problems you're facing, personally or professionally. There are some mentors who will see you in full, who can help you shape the problem from the inside out. They'll help you understand what your strengths and weaknesses are, and what you need to do in order to capitalise and build on those strengths, and help bridge the gaps where your weaknesses are holding you back. Other mentors will be more analytical, or perhaps more focused on the specific problem at hand. The personal and growth issues are not so much of a concern to them (not because they don't care, but because it's not their strength), and so you'll find they'll be there to help you tackle specific problems.

What a mentor looks like

A mentor is someone who has walked where you want to walk, so they can guide you on your journey. They've been around the block, and have insights, wisdom and street smarts to share. Mentors are people who have been successful at something, but that doesn't always mean material success. It can be spiritual achievements, interpersonal skills or having mastered a craft. Maybe it's marketing, or presenting, or an art form. They can be older or younger than you, any race, religion or waist size, or *Star Wars* or *Star Trek* fans.

Being in business, I've naturally sought out successful business-people from whom I've wanted to learn, and whose accountability I've wanted. But often you can find that the right mentor is next door, or maybe it's a family friend or relative.

If you feel awkward asking for a potential mentor's time, remember that people who are successful want to give back. Everyone has gone through a hard time building their careers/ passions, and they are guaranteed to have had multiple people help them on the way. No-one gets there on their own. They'll be grateful for the mentors who helped them, and will most likely enjoy the opportunity to be able to pay it forward to you. Great mentors are the ones who recognise that upon reaching the top, it's wise to help others move up.

An example of great mentorship is how my chairman helped me through doing a massive deal with one of Australia's largest listed companies. He had run a billion-dollar company before, so he knew what this deal would mean for our company—both the good and the bad. He was the one telling me, 'Mick, don't do the deal unless it's right for us'. 'Mick, watch out. The culture might change.' 'Be careful, Mick, they're going to demand this, and that. And soon you'll be in their office, which is likely to make the company become slow, no longer dynamic and agile.' Him being there to keep it all in perspective, with not only the positives of the deal, but with what to be wary of, was the best help to make the big changes successful. You need to truly know where you want to be in your future, and then surround yourself with the type of people who have been there or are on a similar path.

Back yourself, but it's wise to get mentored if you want to accelerate.

TAKE A MOMENT

Who are the experts in your area that you would love to learn from? Write down a list of people you know, and people you know of, who would be great mentors you would love to work with. For example, say you're studying law and there's a certain lawyer you would love to learn from, and then there's that person you've met in the lift once before who you would really, really love to learn from. And let's say that as well as law, you're interested in social enterprises, and you've had an idea for a social enterprise you could be part of to help make law more accessible to those who normally can't afford a lawyer, and think about who, in that field too, you could learn great things from.

Once you have a list of people, divide them into One Year and Five Year categories. The One Year list is people you could reach out to today, and the Five Year list is people who you can't reach out to right now, but who you'll be able to connect with if you progress to where you want to go.

ONE YEAR	FIVE YEAR

How to reach out

If you're wanting to be mentored by someone you don't currently know or have any connections with, the internet is your friend. I've spent ages scouring the internet to find a person's email address, or if that's failed, I've guessed it. See if you can find the formula for the email addresses at their work, and then put in their name and see if it works. You can also find them on LinkedIn: ask to connect and send them an InMail.

Write an upfront, friendly message so there's no pressure on them and it's clear you're not trying to sell them anything—all you're asking for is a chat.

> Hey X, my name's Mick Spencer. I'm the CEO of this emerging company doing X, Y and Z. I've followed your journey and have been very inspired by it. I'm fortunate enough to have been surrounded by some great people and I've learned a lot from people like you.
>
> I have a few questions about X. I'd love to make a time to chat if you have the time. I'm happy to come to you whenever is convenient.
>
> Thanks,
>
> Mick

If they respond that they're willing to catch up, it's important to have a clear idea of what you want out of the meeting. You need to walk in that door knowing exactly what your desired outcomes are. Do you want to just meet this person and ask a specific question, or do you want ongoing mentorship? Could they help you get your dream job, once you know each other well? Or do you have something on the table for them that you think they'd like to know about?

A few years ago, David Jones approached us to make the running singlets for their staff for the Mother's Day Classic. I asked the lady in HR, 'Do you mind if I get access to your CEO, if he's wearing our product?' She replied, 'Oh no, I can't give away his details'. But I knew he would be running in our gear at the Mother's Day Classic, so the day after the event I sent him a LinkedIn request.

> Hi Paul, you used my products yesterday. I'm the 25-year-old CEO of ONTHEGO®. I love what you've done with David Jones. I'd love to meet one day. Would you have time for a coffee? Mick

He didn't answer. A month later I wrote to him again, but received no reply. So a month later I copied and pasted my message again, and I got a reply!

'Sorry about the delay. Sure, I've got time on Tuesday. 30 minutes.'

'I'll be there.'

It was pretty daunting meeting Paul Zahra. He was in charge of a billion-dollar retail store. But I made myself stay cool and focus on what I could learn. He's a great guy who's had a very interesting journey, and I was full of questions. At the end of the 30 minutes he said he'd love to keep in touch. It so happened that a month later he left David Jones and had some more free time, and he reached out saying, 'Hey Mick, how are you going? I've got some time. I'd love to help you out.' I was blown away! I gratefully accepted, and he helped me structure the business for our first capital raise.

When someone agrees to mentor you, it's important you have clear expectations upfront.

What are we in it for?

You're in it to learn and develop, but what about them? You want it to be a win–win. Are you paying them for their mentorship, or are they giving their time for free and ticking their charity box by giving back?

What are we doing?

Make sure you've got a routine. Do you catch up every month? In person, or on Skype? Make sure it's booked in advance, with an expectation of it always happening at that time—no running around rescheduling. You want your mentor to know what you're going to talk about before each conversation, so when you're sending the calendar invite, set an agenda. And are they also available for ad hoc calls?

How long for?

How long are they willing to mentor you for? I've had mentors from as little as six months to as long as two years.

When is it time to move on?

A few times I've realised after six months that it was time to move on. I was preparing a lot before each meeting, and they weren't taking it all in. They didn't really understand what I was asking. It was time to move on because I wasn't getting any benefit. We were just going through the motions. They need to be really invested in the mentorship, otherwise they won't give you helpful advice. You need to have the feeling that they're present, and really hearing you and understanding your questions. Maybe I had outgrown them, or maybe they were distracted by other projects (which is totally understandable)—either way, it's important to end the mentorship well.

You'll find that sometimes they will end it. 'You know, Mick, you don't need me anymore. I love you, but you're ready to go out there on your own now. Let's catch up sometime.' However, sometimes you'll be ready to move on but your mentor may still have knowledge that they want to pass on. If that happens, what do you do? Remember to be grateful. A mentor has taken their precious time to pass on what they've learned. Express your gratitude through words and whatever gesture you're comfortable with and think is appropriate: a gift, a dinner out or something thoughtful. Along with that gratitude, kindly tell them you're ready to move on. Remember, we're all adults here. Even teachers need to be reminded by their students when to allow them to think for themselves, and move on.

Have someone to answer to

One of the challenges of independent work or entrepreneurship is getting caught in the 'blue sky' and being distracted by the world of 'bright, shiny lights'. It doesn't matter how powerful or successful you are, if you want to maintain that level you have to answer to someone. History is littered with examples of people in power who surrounded themselves with yes-men, which caused havoc for themselves and others.

I answer to my chairman and my executive team. My chairman is my boss, and we employ him to be that for me. His job is to make the company focus on our core competencies and priorities, which we've mapped out together as an executive team. He holds me accountable to those core competencies and priorities, and he's also there for key things that pop up and I need guidance on.

My executive team and I are really tight-knit too. I employ three executives—one in each of commerce, finance and merchandise—and they run the day-to-day business now. I'm still involved, but a lot less than I once was. We're like family, and we all answer to each other, though technically they report to me. But because we're all reporting to the board, we all answer to our chairman.

As well as having people to answer to, to hold you accountable and keep you on track, it's important you answer to yourself. It needs to come from within. If you're not disciplined enough to want to answer to someone properly, you're not answering to yourself.

ROUNDUP

- Part of doing an excellent job is knowing what the process is and then improving on it by making it as simple and straightforward as possible.
- When you're working with others, it's important to be a team player. You have to support each other professionally and personally because you go through so much together.
- If you have a mentor, you have a second perspective in your head when it comes to making decisions, which gives you an opportunity to learn from other people's mistakes and successes.
- If you feel awkward asking for a potential mentor's time, remember that great, successful mentors want to give back and help others move up.
- When you find a mentor, set clear mentoring guidelines upfront.
- It's important to have people who hold you accountable and on track, and who you have to answer to; it's also important to answer to yourself.

THE WORST
DECISION
IS THE ONE YOU
DON'T MAKE

THE BEST
DECISION
*IS THE ONE
YOU MAKE*

CHAPTER 11
STREET SMARTS

What I've learned is, many of the most successful entrepreneurs, artists and individuals had little or only some formal education. Some came from absolutely nothing, while others came from upper-middle-class backgrounds. Most of these men and women applied street smarts to get ahead.

Applying street smarts to your career or business practices and habits will take you far, and is something that I believe is totally underutilised. For some people, 'street smarts'—or 'the hustle', as I sometimes call it—might seem underhanded, conjuring up images of drug deals. But to me, being street smart means thinking fast on your feet, understanding human nature, being loyal, being cool and focused, and keeping in mind that everyone is looking out for themselves. I look at examples like my father. Everything he learned that has made him successful came from learning on the street—not from studying. It may sound unconventional, but when you ask someone one year out of university if university is different from their applied work, their answer is usually 'Absolutely yes!'

Think fast on your feet

Starting before you're ready and keeping up the hustle means you have to think fast. In the first *Indiana Jones* movie, one of the characters asks Indiana what's next in their plan. 'I don't know, I'm making this up as I go along', he answers. When you're building your own path, there's no boss but you. You might be employed and have a boss, but they're not responsible for growing your career and achieving your goals. You are. 'The buck', as US President Harry Truman knew, 'stops here'. You're the decision maker, and when it comes down to it you have to make sometimes stressful, lightning-fast decisions. Yes, you'll have the help of mentors and associates, friends and family, but the responsibility is yours. The more you get used to facing big decisions, and seeing the bigger picture pros and cons clearly rather than being lost in the details, the more confidence you'll gain. Those who keep it simple and act fast are the ones who get ahead.

As CEO and executives, we have to think on our feet every day. Recently I had planned to spend a full afternoon on important business, and at noon one of my sales reps said, 'They just got back to us. You can meet the owner of NBL [the National Basketball League] this afternoon'. I instantly responded, 'Okay, cool. Where have I got to be to meet him?' Meeting him was very important for long-term results, so I made the quick decision to sacrifice the meetings I'd planned for that afternoon to make it happen. You need to be able to make lightning decisions, particularly when you know they'll pave the way for the future. The more clarity you have on your professional and personal priorities, the quicker you'll be able make decisions because you'll instantly be able to analyse what matters most to you.

People can get paralysed when making a decision because they're worried they'll make the wrong decision, and they try to avoid doing that at all costs. But the worst decision is the one you don't make. Yes, if you have the time to think it through, cross the t's and dot the i's. If you have concerns you need to talk through, take the decision to the right person who is qualified to give advice. Too many people spend too long in the grey area, unsure what to do. Don't dwell on things. Make a decision and move forward. The best decision is *the one you make*. Taking action is the best decision, and through action you make it the right decision.

Understanding human nature

By nature I'm an eternal optimist. I always have been, and I'm sure I always will be! So when OTG began, I was very trusting, and when I met someone who wanted to work with me I thought, 'Amazing! That'd be great!' My trusting nature has opened doors for me as a networker and businessperson, but it has also interfered with my gut instinct. I've been let down by people a lot, more often than I can remember, and I've made the mistake of trusting the wrong people. At least every instance of adversity and challenge has paved the way for me to have a stronger mind, and taught me a stark lesson in human nature. I'm a lot more cautious now. You get a bit less optimistic as you get wiser, though I do believe it's good to stay optimistic.

The professional and business world can be dog eat dog at times. Everybody's been burned at some point—if not multiple times. Sadly, it seems to be part of the game. You need to recognise this early on, and build your 'trust circle' early on. This is a must.

Two years into OTG I was advised to hire a general manager. 'You need to get someone to help run the day-to-day, so you can get out and do what you do best.' I met a great guy who was in his early 40s, and he took a big risk by coming to work for me. I'm sure I was paying him nowhere near the money he could have earned elsewhere, and he was based in Queensland so he was travelling to Canberra regularly for work. We had a good relationship and I gave him a fair amount of autonomy in the business, both in the running of things and with my finance guy. After some months I realised that a few transactions were not matching up in the reconciliation of accounts, and when I looked deeper I realised he was taking out personal expenses that I wasn't approving and that I had no visibility on. I asked him about it, and he couldn't answer me straight. I told him, 'You've broken my values about being open and honest. If you had come to me and talked about it, it would be a different story. But you've done this behind my back'. I fired him that day. OTG lost about $20 000 over a few months as a result of these expenses. Being a small business that was just getting off the ground, it almost broke us. I learned this was also my stupid fault for not having the mechanisms or tools to ensure goals were being met. I'm sure he meant well and it wasn't the right fit, but it never feels good.

Today I understand human nature: everyone has their own agenda, as they should. It's something I often pose to my team: What are you aiming to get out of this? Where do you want to be in three to five years? How can you use me to get ahead? And I keep in mind that their agenda will not always be in alignment with my company's agenda. It's natural in business for it to not always work out for people. That's fine. I've had to develop the skill of properly listening to my gut. It's one of the key attributes my father taught us kids—'always trust your gut instinct'—but I had to make a few mistakes to fine-tune it. Today, my gut is my first and foremost decision-making tool. I hire and fire off it, from staff and shareholders to friends and acquaintances. Sometimes the nicest person in the world is the one who screws you the most.

Learn to look for signs, ask for advice and don't be afraid to end a professional relationship early on before it develops into something that can threaten you. If you fine-tune your gut, you'll win in the long run.

Be loyal

One of the most—if not *the* most—valued virtues held by those on the streets, whether it's a hustler in Los Angeles or a Mafioso in Sicily, is loyalty. Loyalty is what saves lives in their work, and in the professional world it can save careers and businesses. Loyalty carries people through the hard times, and propels them in the good times. Those you are loyal to, and who repay you with their own loyalty, will help you weather storms, provide their insights and street smarts, and can help you with your blind spots. Whether they're family, a trusted colleague, a mentor or a friend, these people will have your back and you'll have theirs. Now I'm lucky. I have loyal people close. I've been loyal to them and they to me. It's a real-deal, super great feeling.

The world is changing and people are somewhat less loyal now than they used to be because they have more options available to them. It's making loyalty even more important. The challenge with us Millennials is that we want to have everything quickly. We want to make a big difference in our jobs in six months. We want to feel important in a year. We want to feel love in a month. But life doesn't work that way; everything that's good takes time. And loyalty takes time to build. But once there, loyal people will see you through thick and thin.

I have a staff member who joined our team after begging me for six months for an internship. I didn't have the time to take him on at first, but after six months of him hustling I said, 'Okay, let's get you started as an intern. You can start building out some databases for me'. He's a very smart and driven guy from Pakistan with a Master's Degree in Finance and a Bachelor's Degree in Finance and Business Economics, and yet he was thrilled. After six months of being an intern he was begging me for a job. 'Yep, I love your work,' I said, 'let's make it happen.' So I created a job for him. Over the next six months he quickly learned everything about working in our production area, so we moved him into a production role. He was loyal to me and I was loyal to him. Today he's a middle manager kicking goals for us. He could have earned a lot more money and been provided more opportunities elsewhere in the short term, but we gave him this path, created roles for him, and he is massively thankful and loyal. After two and a half years with us we began sponsoring him on a visa to become a permanent resident of Australia, which is massive for him. His parents are over the moon he's getting permanent residency, and he's stoked that he's proving to everyone back home that he can make it. And he can. He'll do anything for his teammates at OTG, as would we for him. Over two and a half years he progressed further and was promoted more than most, and it's because of his great work and his loyalty. He will inevitably be very, very successful with or without us. These are the stories of why I love doing what we do.

Be cool. Be calm. Be focused.

On the street and in the boardroom, it's good to be cool under pressure. You need to look at things differently, and occasionally have a laugh. If you're into sport you'll know that the best of the best win not because they don't make mistakes—they win because they're *calm and focused under pressure*. It's the battle of the mind meeting reality, and it's where they thrive. Think of Tiger Woods when he was on the eighteenth hole and down two strokes and came back to win, or Roger Federer when he was at game point to win the set at Wimbledon... You can see the look in their eyes: it's as if everything around them disappears, and their sole focus is the shot. It's a meditative state that can be achieved with practice, and it applies to the boardroom, a job interview, asking for a promotion and doing a deal just as much as it does on the green or the court.

That level of focus is all in the mind, and the great news is we can train our minds to do it—Tiger Woods and Roger Federer weren't born with it, they learned it. Anxiety is normal, and controlling anxiety is totally possible. That's not to say the required level of focus is easily achieved—but countless individuals achieve it every day. Your fear will still be there, but it'll be under control. That's what the athlete, the surgeon, the musician, the CEO and the street-smart person understands. Fear is normal; defeating it takes willpower and practice; and nothing worth winning or achieving comes without its own set of struggles, obstacles and doses of fear. For me the blessing of having a serious heart condition, as well as severe short-sighted eyesight, taught me from a young age how to be calm in stressful situations. When you're 17 and your heart is beating at 240 beats per minute, panicking is the least helpful thing to get your heart rate down again. I'd have to calm myself, focus on the beats and watch the time to know if I'd need to go to hospital.

Be cool and focused, and you'll be ahead of the game. A great saying to remember is look and act like the dumbest and most 'chilled' in the room—then you can attack much better.

Put yourself first—it's not a bad thing

Keep in mind that everyone is looking out for themselves. This doesn't mean that everybody is inherently selfish, but it does mean we're hardwired for self-preservation. The decisions we make boil down to, 'What's in it for me?', or 'What's in it for me and the people I represent or care about?' Even charitable organisations have to be selfish—they fight for dollars for their dependants that might otherwise go elsewhere.

Putting yourself first in your life is important because if you don't put yourself first, no-one else will. It's really about respect. Too many people don't do this in their jobs, in their relationships and in their ideals. Love to another is most possible by those who love themselves first. Just as parents manage to take some time for themselves so they're replenished and can be there emotionally for the family. To be able to feed others, you first need to be fed. And once you're fed, you'll have the energy to help others. Putting yourself first shows you respect yourself, are proud of what you're doing and want to be able to give back.

Begging, borrowing and stealing

Let's look at the three aspects of street smarts that are not so virtuous: begging, borrowing and stealing. Now, I'm not advocating you do any of these (apart from borrow), but let's turn these three tools of the street-smart hustler on their head for a moment and see how they can be used wisely.

Begging

Instead of begging, let's call it persistence. Sometimes people won't return your calls or emails. Everybody's busy. Perhaps they're leaving their position and are yet to announce it, or maybe there's a new deal in the works that you haven't been privy to. In my experience, it's always best to persist. If getting hold of them is worth the effort and time, keep knocking on doors, calling, emailing and making sure that whoever you're trying to reach doesn't forget about you. Never ever settle. Persist. The best sales guys I have never stop.

Borrowing

Let's forget the financial aspect of borrowing for a moment, and instead think about borrowing... ideas. In art, borrowing (and outright stealing!) has been going on since time began. Why reinvent the wheel if you can take the geniuses' ideas, add significant value and prosper? In business, ideas are everywhere. Don't think that because somebody else is doing something, you can't. You can borrow their idea and make it unique, playing on your own strengths.

I saw McDonald's design-your-own burgers, and from that I invented OTG's customisation station for apparel. It has helped OTG lead the way in innovation without building something brand new. I'd had an increasing number of customers who wanted to interact physically with our product, rather than only be able to design their garments online. They wanted to feel the fabrics and see the colours in person. At the same time, I was having conversations with retailers who wanted to offer something like custom-made apparel or uniforms in stores. So I created a digital tablet that goes with a garment rack where people could touch and feel the fabrics and try them on. They literally design their own product in store, at a kiosk. OTG's customisation stations are currently launching in Australia, and they mean we'll be able to continually scale around the country without having to open our own stores. It's offering customers the really cool experience they want, and is bringing something new and inventive to the marketplace.

Stealing

Innovation, in many ways, is improving on existing ideas. Those ideas are shared, or some would say they're stolen. In the world of personal computers the idea of having a mouse was groundbreaking. In fact, when Steve Jobs first saw it, he jumped around the room shouting, 'Why aren't you doing anything with this? This is the greatest thing. This is revolutionary!' Steve Jobs saw the mouse on a tour of Xerox (which he had hustled and negotiated to get). And Xerox had originally 'stolen' the idea for a mouse from a Stanford Research Institute researcher, Douglas Engelbart, and made some improvements on it themselves.

Many people have accused Bill Gates of stealing from Steve Jobs, and Steve Jobs of stealing from Xerox. In an 'Ask Me Anything' on Reddit (which is an online social news, content rating and discussion website), Bill Gates was plainly asked, 'Did you copy Steve Jobs or did he copy you?' His reply was: 'The main "copying" that went on relative to Steve and me is that we both benefited from the work that Xerox Parc did in creating graphical interface ... Steve hired Bob Belleville, I hired Charles Simonyi. We didn't violate any IP rights Xerox had'.

Or, put another way, in Walter Isaacson's biography of Steve Jobs he reported that when Jobs first accused Gates by saying, 'I trusted you, and now you're stealing from us!', Gates replied, 'Well, Steve, I think there's more than one way of looking at it.

I think it's more like we both had this rich neighbour named Xerox and I broke into his house to steal the TV set and found out that you had already stolen it'.

Today people are innovating more than ever before, with things constantly being improved. If you see an idea that you think can be done better, like Steve Jobs when he saw the mouse, get out there and innovate.

ROUNDUP

- Being street smart means thinking fast on your feet, understanding human nature, being loyal, being cool and focused, and keeping in mind that everyone is looking out for themselves.
- To get ahead you need to keep it simple and act fast.
- Make a decision and move forward. By taking action you make it the right decision.
- It's essential to build your 'trust circle' early on. Sometimes the nicest person in the world is the one who screws you the most.
- Loyalty takes time to build. But once there, loyal people will see you through thick and thin.
- On the street and in the boardroom, you have to be cool under pressure and remain focused.
- Fear is normal. Defeating it takes willpower and practice and nothing worth winning or achieving comes without its own set of struggles, obstacles and doses of fear.
- Everyone is looking out for themselves. The decisions we make boil down to 'What's in it for me?'
- If you see an idea that you think can be done better, get out there and innovate.

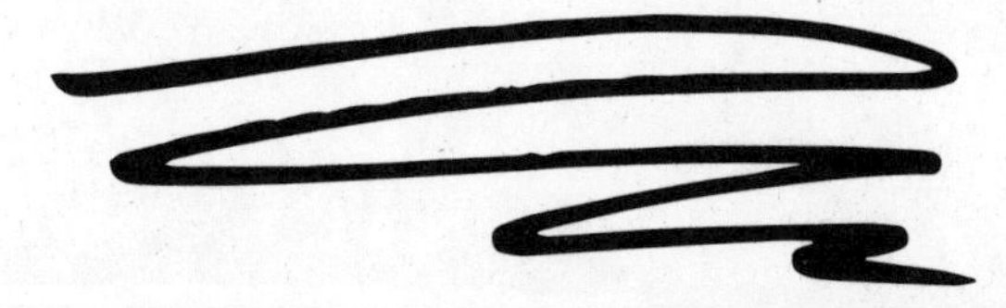

THE WORLD WAS BUILT
ON OTHER PEOPLE'S
RULES
QUESTION THEM
BREAK THEM
MAKE YOUR
OWN RULES

CHAPTER 12
WHAT IT TAKES

What does it really take to achieve our dreams? To envision and design our lives, and then make those dreams happen? It takes constantly checking in with your habits, and constantly pushing the boundaries. It's making mistakes fast and moving on fast. When you're building something significant, you're constantly dealing with stresses, and constantly worrying, 'Am I doing the right job? Am I okay? Am I developing quickly enough? Can I handle it? Do I have the right people around me? Do we have enough cash to fund where we need to go? Is the team happy? Is this what I'll continue to love doing?'

It takes being able to deal with too many things piling up at once. If you want to grow by 100 per cent, 300 per cent and 500 per cent, like we have, things pile up regularly. You must get used to mess, uncertainty and things breaking. When you're that ambitious, you're never settled. You're in a constant state of pushing the limits, and it can be very exhausting. You're a lot more stressed and you're living with a lot more pressure. But hey, what a ride! You only live once.

There will be times when you're too under the pump and you negotiate to tame it back for a week or a month — to rejuvenate so you can push hard again. But there will be other times when it's too much stress, too big of a workload or you're simply utterly exhausted, and you'll have to push through to deliver. That's when you'll have to dig deep.

Digging deep

We've all had those moments. It's 4 am and you have an early flight. You have deadlines and you're feeling unwell. The alarm clock goes off telling you to go to the gym and you simply don't want to. I see so many amazing people push through, such as single parents I employ continuing to evolve their careers. They dig deep all the time and I respect them so much. Digging deep is *never* easy. It's the overseas flight where I'm on the ground for three days, and I've got to meet a client and do a presentation and look like I've got it all figured out. I'm jet-lagged, have barely slept, and I've got to make sure that everything is dialled back home, or I've got to handle some problems that occurred while I was flying over. Then I've got to get up at what is 2 am for my body clock and have as much energy as I normally would if I'd slept well.

I have countless stories like this, where I've had to really dig deep. In OTG's third year we got an overseas charity as a client who needed 10 000 drink bottles. They transferred $25 000 upfront for the drink bottles, we checked that the funds had cleared and then we began manufacturing. At that time OTG's cash flow was tight, and it was great to have this order come through to ease the financial stress. The charity sent us the details of a freight-forwarding company they had used often — there's a lot of freight forwarding in our industry, a lot of one-man operators who you pay and they control the cargo ships, and so on. We transferred $13 000 in freight cost to the freight-forwarding company and shipped the drink bottles. We then got a message from the bank to say that the $25 000 transfer was done with a stolen credit card, and we had to pay it all back immediately. We panicked, looked deeper into the freight-forwarding company and realised it and the charity was a hoax. They had run off with the $13 000 'freight' money. I had to negotiate like crazy with the bank to only pay half of the $25 000 back immediately, and pay the rest back in monthly instalments because now the business was *really* struggling. Moments like these almost sent us broke, and there have been many more. But it was always the way we looked at them that made the change.

Winston Churchill said, 'Success consists of going from failure to failure without loss of enthusiasm'. It took us six months to get our heads back above water—back to where we'd been six months earlier. It was a kick in the gut to not only lose the money but to lose the six months of growth. I had to sell hard, working even harder than before. It was a painfully stressful six months. I was negotiating with all of our internal suppliers, letting them know what had happened. 'Guys, we've had a big problem. Can I pay your bill a month later?' I was totally transparent, communicating with them so they knew what was happening. And because I'd built my relationship with them over the previous three years, and I'd always done the right thing by them, they understood. 'Sure thing Mick, that's fine.'

Through most of this journey I've dealt with a lot of pain. I've felt totally alone many times. Ultimately, the buck stops with me and my team; it's all resting on our shoulders; it's all our responsibility. I have only gotten to where I am today through my commitment to my purpose; it's my purpose that's helped me to dig deep every time. To make your dreams happen will be hard, hard work. To live your purpose every day will be painful at times. You'll have to dig deep. And when you feel like you have nothing left—absolutely nothing—you'll have to dig even deeper. But when your heart is beating with purpose, when you have a vision and a mission you're turning into a reality, when you see how you're touching people's lives, when you look after yourself with great habits, you'll find that somehow, you can do it.

Recently, I had eight flights and visited five cities and four hotels in two weeks. I spent only 24 hours in my own bed at home in Canberra. A friend—a lovely 29-year-old guy—committed suicide on the weekend before I had to leave. I couldn't believe it. I was shattered that he was gone. On the Thursday morning, I woke up in Canberra and had an 8 am flight to Melbourne. I had three back-to-back meetings booked in from 10 am to noon. At 1.30 pm I would be giving my fourth presentation for the week, and I would have to nail it. It was the last piece of the puzzle to close our biggest deal yet, with one of Australia's largest listed companies, and all their executives would be at the presentation. They'd be thinking, 'Mick has sold us well over the past three months. Now, can he deliver a presentation in front of 200 of our staff, who will be the ones selling his products when the deal goes through?' I had to tick a lot of boxes. My presentation had to make the executives want to do the deal, and it had to get the buy-in from their salespeople so they would effectively sell our products in the future. To do that I had to make sure I was presenting OTG in a way that wouldn't look like a threat to them, and would instead look like the opportunity it is. It was full on—there was a lot of light on Mick. It was all up to me to perform well.

At 6 am that morning in Canberra I was thinking about the presentation I had to give in Melbourne that afternoon, which I still needed to prepare for. In a perfect world I would have had all week to prepare for something that crucial, but I'd already taken flights and delivered three different presentations that week.

I went to the gym before my flight, the first time in a while I'd managed to go, which was my own fault. In my overly busy schedule of the previous few weeks I'd struggled to make it happen. At my gym there's a big TV screen on the wall, showing everyone's heart rate percentages in the gym. Everyone's rate is around 60 per cent or 70 per cent, and then mine shot up to 200 per cent. You could almost see my T-shirt rattling, and if you'd felt my chest you'd have thought, 'Holy shit…!' It scares people around me more than it scares me now.

I immediately realised that I shouldn't have pushed myself so hard. I knew that I was overworked and hadn't had enough sleep. When I look after my body my heart is fine, but now it had gone off into SVT. I stopped what I was doing and headed straight to the bathroom where I could have peace and quiet. I got a towel, wet it, and lay it across my neck. With SVT you have to be calm—panicking makes it worse. I've had my heart go off when I've been hiking mountains in China without phone reception—a non–English speaking place. I've had it go off in 40-degree heat when I was riding my bike on Rottnest Island, just off Perth, again without phone reception. I've had it go into SVT when I was snowboarding in Whistler, and going for a run in the European winter. While being really calm I either have to do a Valsalva manoeuvre, which involves breathing really hard into my diaphragm and pushing hard to get my heart to drop back to my normal rhythm, or have a freezing cold shower to shock it back. The third option is kind of dangerous, but they also suggest you can just run *hard*.

I calmly breathed hard into my diaphragm, and managed to shock it back into its normal rhythm. Now it was 6.30 am and I was utterly exhausted. SVT takes everything out of you and takes more than a day to recover from. Great. I had such a big day ahead.

I got my things and headed home, and then straight to the airport, to find out that my 8 am flight was cancelled. 'Shit.' I like energy and momentum; I hate it when a cancelled flight keeps me stuck in an airport when I'm meant to be in another city in meetings. They put me on a 9.30 am flight, and I asked my EA, Deb, to let all my meetings for that morning know I wouldn't be able to make it. Waiting in the lounge at the airport, I pulled out my laptop and worked on my presentation for that afternoon.

I finally landed and got into Melbourne CBD at 11 am, tired as hell, really lacking my usual GO GO energy. This happens a lot. Adrenal fatigue, and lack of mojo. The past two weeks' hectic schedule had taken its toll. My friend committing suicide had crushed me. And my heart going into SVT had drained all the last bits of energy I'd had. There was no amount of coffee or food that would help—it was adrenal fatigue and simple exhaustion, both emotional and physical. I began to feel emotionally overwhelmed and unable to think straight, which gets me anxious and in the shits. I was thinking, 'I'm an amazing guy with an amazing brain. What's going on? I'm not my usual self. I have to get out of this. I don't like it'.

Being that exhausted started to awaken my self-doubt. 'Can I pull off this presentation? How can I get on stage in two hours and be full of energy and nail it? I just don't think I can do it ...' In moments like this you've got to decide: Am I going to do it, or not? I decided I was going to do it. I wasn't going to cancel our biggest deal yet—a deal that would propel OTG forward like nothing else could! I was lucky I had Michael, my 2IC and Chief Commercial Officer, with me. I turned to him and admitted, 'I'm completely stuffed. I'm going to really struggle'. He replied, 'Mate, I'll be at your back. It's fine. You'll nail it. We're gonna wipe them out'. This is why it's so important to have great people around you.

I had to dig deep, really deep. I had to rejuvenate myself. I listened to some good music that I like, and then I had a shower to help me feel refreshed and clean after the flight. And I simply forced myself to shake it off. I sang really loudly, did some push-ups and then gazed out the window at the view. I have a favourite saying: 'You can't be half pregnant'. You can't go in there half-assed. I believe in doing things at a 100 per cent. As my chairman says (and has written on my forehead), 'Never leave anything on the table and leave no stone unturned'. I was going to nail this! I thought about my message and my purpose, and decided that Mick Spencer was going to captivate the audience, delivering an ace presentation. They didn't know I'd had a bad day, and a big two weeks. They didn't know I was tired. So I made the decision to really, really dig deep. And I did. I've studied NLP and I have some rituals I do to help get my mind in the zone, putting on certain clothes and a certain watch, and not looking at anything on my phone.

The moment I was in the zone, I was on, all in, no looking back. I'd had no sleep and everything else, but I was in the zone. It's addictive and exhilarating knowing you're in control—you're the master of your own destiny, your own mind and body.

I did the presentation, and I nailed it. The deal has since been closed! Afterwards there was a dinner, which I went to so I could speak with all of the salespeople face to face. I was still in the zone, still digging deep, still drawing on energy from somewhere inside. I spoke passionately with every person there that night, staying until the end. The company's leaders all left between 8.30 and 9 pm, which was well after the dinner had ended and totally respectable. But I went the extra mile, giving it my all, making sure I spoke with everyone, staying until the last person left.

Go the extra mile

Going the extra mile always pays off. Always. For my very first order, I didn't just deliver those soccer shirts wrapped in plastic. I bought beautiful boxes, I packaged them nicely and I personally delivered them. When I was reaching out to Paul, who at the time was the CEO of David Jones, I didn't stop when he didn't reply. I sent him the same message a second time. And, a month later, a third time. I would have kept it up all year if he hadn't replied. When I didn't have money for hotels, I didn't simply not go to expos. I slept in my car and sold hard at the expos. On that Thursday night, after the toughest day of having to dig extra deep, I didn't go home at 9 pm once the dinner was finished and the other business leaders were leaving. I stayed back until the end, and made sure I had personally spoken and connected with every sales representative. They're all much more inspired and excited to sell our products because I took the time to personally connect (granted, I don't yet have kids to go home to, so I still have the luxury of being able to stay out late).

Going the extra mile takes effort, energy and time. It's why so few people do it, and why you'll stand out from the crowd if you do. I go the extra mile because what I'm building is bigger than myself. I see OTG as very important for many people. We're providing jobs and opportunities for 35 staff and for over 1000 factory workers across the seven key factories we use every day. We're keeping customers super happy. And we're changing an industry day by day.

***

In 2014, I was on the phone with a client, hoping to close a big order for IRONMAN®. She said, 'Mick, you know, I think OTG is great, but I don't know if you know the market well enough. You've never even competed in a triathlon, let alone an IRONMAN®, so how can you assure me the product is the right fit for our customer? Who has tested it?' She was right, I hadn't, and maybe if I had firsthand experience I would know my market base better. The World IRONMAN® Championships in Kona, Hawaii—the famous, hardest race in the world—had been on TV that Sunday. After watching it I went out and ran 20 kilometres. Until that day I had never run more than 10 kilometres! It had inspired me so much it doubled my running distance. It looked like such an exciting event, and I wanted to be a part of that feeling!

'I'll tell you what,' I replied, 'if I do the event—if I compete in the upcoming Canberra IRONMAN®—will you give me the order?'

She chuckled. 'Sure, Mick, I promise. If you do the IRONMAN®, you'll get the order.'

I grinned. 'It's a deal.'

It was nine weeks until the IRONMAN® race day in Canberra, and people normally train for six months to do an IRONMAN®. Everyone thought I was mad—I had never even done a small triathlon! It was going to be mentally, emotionally and physically challenging, especially because of my heart condition and my eyesight (my contacts don't agree with water, so I would have to wear goggles with the risk of them slipping, and then no longer being able to see underwater). I had never swum more than 1 kilometre, and in this specific IRONMAN® I had to swim 3.1 kilometres. I had never cycled more than 100 kilometres, and now I had to ride 130 kilometres. I'd only just run my first 20-kilometre run, and on race day I would have to run 29.2 kilometres—and I'd have to do the three parts consecutively, in 40-degree heat. There was no way I could train my body and gain the endurance needed to compete... or was there?

Nelson Mandela said, 'It always seems impossible until it's done'. I prioritised training, and made time for it around running OTG. I immediately bought a wetsuit and completed a small triathlon that first weekend. I was starting before I was ready to the max! I would wake up at 5 am to swim before getting into the office, and I'd run or ride every evening—every single day. I put up big posters on my wall: '9 weeks to go', '8 weeks to go', and so on. It also said, 'Run your arse off. Ride your legs off. Swim your hands off. Eat, sleep, work hard and you'll make it'. You have no idea just how much you're truly capable of doing, achieving and making happen in this life. Starting before you're ready means making a commitment to push yourself beyond your perceived limits. You're capable of achieving the things you've dreamed of... and more.

During those two months of training and working I completely exhausted myself, and after the IRONMAN® I was burned out. But I'd done it! I'd surprised myself, and I was proud of what I'd accomplished. By making that simple promise, that commitment, I was resourceful and found the impossible becoming possible. I learned how to train my body more efficiently. I gained endurance through long-distance training and I pushed myself so far beyond what I thought possible that it changed me forever. The biggest lesson was the uptake of my mind. I was astonished by what is actually possible if you put your mind to it! Similarly to business, if I could complete an IRONMAN® with just nine weeks of training, from never having done a triathlon before, imagine what we can all do if we put our minds to it...

Plus, as a bonus, I got the order! Which taught me a powerful lesson: when you commit to something, or commit something to somebody, it's not just about you anymore. It's about something greater. And when you reach your goal, you look back and wonder, 'If this is possible, then what else is?'

Put in the extra hour of work to make your presentation go from good to outstanding. Spend every Saturday morning learning a key skill that will help you go the extra mile at work. Spend the time that you're driving to strategise on who would be a great mentor, and how you can reach out to them to get their attention.

If you live deliberately with great habits, seek out mentors, constantly educate and upskill yourself, you're going the extra mile. Do it, and you'll reach your goals much sooner.

Other people's rules

Sir Richard Branson once said, 'You don't learn to walk by following rules. You learn by doing, and by falling over'. And remember that Steve Jobs said, 'everything around you that you call life, was made up by people that were no smarter than you. And you can change it, you can influence it, you can build your own things that other people can use'.

All of my life I've broken 'the rules' in order to get to where I am today. The world was built on other people's rules. Question them. Break them. Make your own rules. Move fast and break things. Don't be afraid.

Get it done

I'm a constant lover of the value, 'Get it *done done done*'. This is absolutely crucial. Get it done. Take action. I can't stand hanging around dawdling. I know it can be hard at times to execute your purpose and passions, but who else is going to do it? There are too many people who talk, and too few who actually get things done. I talk, and I back it up with action and results. I love to get up at 4.30 am and be in bed by 11 pm. I get the most out of my days and put my dreams into executable steps that I take action on because I know that nobody else is going to do it for me. You can have support, guidance, people cheering on the sidelines—but you're the one who has to run your race. Which is good, because the only one who can do it right is you!

You may be thinking, 'But Mick, you've already made it. That's easy for you to say'. I've made it? Not yet. I might be able to support myself and I'm growing my business, sure. But what happens if I stop? Everything stops. My dreams are bigger than where I am right now, and I'm willing to work harder and longer to make a bigger difference. Remember, you're never half pregnant.

A partner in crime

We can't do life on our own. Choosing the right life partner is the best decision I've ever made. While building OTG I was also enjoying the single life, dating girls, but none of them were serious. I then met a girl I clicked with, and we dated for 18 months. After the breakup, I was done. I had my company and I didn't want to think about relationships for a pretty long while.

Three weeks later I bumped into Alicia at a bar. We caught up to reconnect the week later, both curious what the other had been doing over the past five years since we'd seen each at the uni lectures I walked out on. We had a ball hanging out, and for the next few weeks went boating together regularly. It was like nothing had changed—we got on so well.

After a few months, we started dating, and after a few more months, I realised that she's the girl I want to marry. I proposed to her on a beach in Hawaii in July 2017, and she said 'Yes!' She was there at the start of my journey with OTG, and now she's with me for the rest of it, and for our amazing future together.

I think it's everyone's dream to find someone they love. Not only is it special, it's super powerful when you know your emotional grounding is cemented. We all need grounding; you can't do everything on your own. I know people who are chasing their careers or business who say, 'I don't have time for a partner', but they don't realise the risk associated with that outlook. I've noticed a huge change in my emotional state now, when I come home to someone I know and trust and love so much. I can do more, I'm more efficient, I've got more of a platform to jump off. When I was running the company and single, it was good in some ways, but it meant that work was all-consuming and I was constantly scatted. Having Alicia, who completely understands me and who I completely understand, and who I'm with on this journey of life, makes the whole journey so much better, so much more fulfilling and less stressful. It ultimately doesn't matter what happens workwise because we will always have each other.

It's been said that out of the CEOs of Fortune 500 companies, 80 per cent are still in their first marriage. That says something about the power of a partner in crime—of having their support—especially if you're taking big risks in your professional life. I love having Alicia's love, support and grounding to come home to.

Here's to your success

To get to where I am today, I've had to maximise every moment. I've faked it until I've made it, connected with my purpose and designed my future, believed in myself, and had to trust that the dots would connect. I've been coachable, been very conscious about building great habits, promoted OTG constantly and backed my talk with action and results. I've faced the tall poppy syndrome and learned how to be unaffected by the naysayers. I've been rejected, I've moved through fear and self-doubt. I've experienced the imposter syndrome often, but haven't let it steer me off my course. I've tried to give 120 per cent each day, lived below my means and sacrificed a lot. I've actively learned new things. I've networked like mad and negotiated heaps, and used social media to my advantage. I've been transparent, sought out great mentors, lived the 4 Ps (Purpose, People, Planet, Profit) passionately, applied street smarts to business, and dug deep constantly.

Nothing on this journey has been easy, but this journey has also meant that I've got to have people like Paul (former CEO of David Jones) and Hap (founder of The North Face) as mentors. Not long ago I upgraded my Toyota to an Aston Martin (it's such a fun car—I love it). Even more exciting is that I've been able to watch staff members shine in the culture we've created. I've been able to give people a better product in one-tenth of the time, with better service. And most exciting of all, I live my dream every day. I'm building my vision. I'm the master of my own destiny—and it's freaky how cool that feels. And, surprisingly, it's all happened very quickly, when you consider the amount of time we're alive.

Though we've come somewhat far, we're still only at the beginning. I really feel like we're just getting started. Where OTG is today is exciting, but I'm more pumped for the future because there's still so much more of this path to run down. My 'success' has taken time. Everything that's a success takes time. It's five or 10 years of blood, sweat, tears and pain for most people to 'make it'. If someone is a multimillionaire or billionaire, chances are it's taken them 10 to 50 years of working insane hours and applying the strategies I've shared in this book, and more, to get there. The risk with us Millennials is that we see time through a warped, unrealistic lens. We want things quickly. But careers, businesses, relationships... they all take time. Building and creating takes time. You won't make it in a year. But if you keep hustling and persisting, keep living deliberately and making smart decisions, you'll make it. I started OTG in 2012, and there's a long roller-coaster ahead. I'm excited for it. I hope you're excited for your upcoming roller-coaster ride, too.

Here's to your success and the next phase—what will be next for you?

WHAT'S NEXT: GOING GLOBAL

As I've alluded to a few times in this book, you never know what conversation will be the next life-changing one—in your career, in your business, in your life.

In early 2017, I made contact with Andrew Banks from *Shark Tank*. We spoke a fair bit and I also formed a great connection with his PA, who was an incredible support base. Coincidentally, both Andrew Banks and Richard Branson mentioned a man to me who had led Virgin's global operations and was coming back to Australia. We connected and he was quite interested in what OTG had to offer.

While he was finding his feet back on home soil, he mentioned he was getting involved in a business that could be a big 'white label' opportunity for us, specifically because of our technology. ('White labelling' is essentially using your software, or your business's product or service, for another brand. For example, most of the auto industry brands are made in the top four car companies' factories. For us it was a great opportunity to reach a bigger audience, and a bigger sales team, and create our products and software for other companies—so they give us the volume and we can focus on what we do best!) That business turned out to be Wesfarmers Ltd, one of Australia's top 10 companies, with tens of billions in market capitalisation. It's the parent company of retailers such as Officeworks, Kmart, Target, Coles and Bunnings. One of its businesses is Workwear Group, Australia's largest and leading uniform company and owner of famous brands Hard Yakka and King Gee, along with NNT (neat and trim) Uniforms.

In the summer of 2017–18, I was introduced to Doug, the CEO of Workwear Group, who knew of OTG via his executive team, which had seen recent press about OTG successfully securing a large contract with Sheffield Wednesday Football Club in the UK. Workwear Group had personal, digital and mass customisation on their agenda, and were questioning how they could better offer experiences to their customers, run their business in the new age and be a lot more digitally efficient. They were immediately interested in our business and our offering, and after a first meeting with them—which my chairman, Chris, attended with me—Chris said, 'Mick, I think we can do really good business with those guys'. He was right. I had a great feeling and was very inspired about the business opportunity.

Shortly after that meeting, I had a call from Doug, the head of the group, who said, 'Mick, you're a lot more visionary and entrepreneurial than I am. You tell us how you think we can do a deal'. And there it was: our first massive opportunity with a really willing and smart partner. You know, in business you knock on so many doors, tender so many jobs and bid for so much work, only to be pulled around and told 'no'. I think it's partly because the level of respect is changing and it's harder in this day and age to trust people's words.

I briefed my board and executive committee at our next gathering and told them why I thought this was a great opportunity for the business. Big company meets small. Small company gets support. Big company gets the nimble offering and service. Great option. For me, it was a big decision to even consider something like this because a large conglomerate can really suck the lifeblood out of you if you're not careful. But it felt right. These guys and girls could really teach us a few things, and vice versa.

We were asked what we needed (financially) to build the platform and get the product to market, and then came up with a commercial model that was passed by Workwear Group.

Next came the exciting moment when we received a letter of intent of partnership. I'd dreamed of this for a long time, and it felt great! I wasn't surprised because we'd spent so much time working so hard on our passion, our product…our dream. But when it becomes a reality, it's a really cool place to be.

Then before we knew it, we'd completed a transaction with one of the country's biggest companies, and it helped to set the bar higher, and higher again. We are now part of Wesfarmers. The moment that deal was underway, I was already working on the next one, keeping innovation and disruption at the forefront.

Keep asking, 'What's next?' Never settle. Never stop having that conversation. Never stop following through with people. Never stop being inspired. You can be amazing, and you know it.

Shoot high, work hard, play hard and have lots of fun!

INDEX

Throughout this index the letters MS signify the author.